Texas Hold'em Poker
Claiming $2-$5

ISBN 0-9705466-1-0

©1996, 1999, 2000 G. Ed Conly

Dedication

This book is dedicated to the memory of my father. From the time I was little, he always told me, "Professional gamblers don't gamble." It was many years before I finally realized to what he was referring. Coming from a man who had rarely placed a single bet, it was extraordinary advice. The truth is that professional gamblers only knowingly *make good bets*. If there is no *probable* edge, there is no bet for a professional. Dad got me started in the right direction, though, and that's what matters. I wish there were opportunities for him to give me more advice.

Acknowledgments

I need to thank Bob Gunner for his excellent editing. Thanks to him this book is both clearer and easier to read. I'd also like to thank my brothers Marc and Craig for their help and input. The list of friends and family that have encouraged me to finish this project would be extremely lengthy, but I thank you one and all.

About the Author

During his brief career in telecommunications, G. Ed Conly spent several years as a recreational poker player, eventually playing professionally as a proposition player for over a year in $2-$5 games. He successfully plays in bigger games when traveling outside of Colorado. In 1998 he won first place in the National Poker Room Employee's limit hold'em tournament in Mesquite, NV, ($5,500 first prize) and has won several other smaller tournaments. He currently deals the game he only really wants to play. He holds a degree in Physics from the University of Colorado.

Table Of Contents

Who Needs This Book?

This book is written for anyone who wants to win consistently at the $2-$5 game that is spread in any number of casinos. Up until now only general and limited information has been available on this type of game. You will want to study this book if:

- You currently cannot consistently win at this game at the $9-$12 (or more) per hour rate. Less if the pot is raked for a jackpot.

- You are a fixed-limit player and travel or play in $2-$5 games on occasion.

- You are seriously considering moving up from a friendly private game to casino play in $2-$5 games.

- You enjoy studying all aspects of poker.

- You are interested in the necessary considerations that apply to all spread-limit games.

- You have a standard deviation significantly above $80 per hour and want to lower it.

Within the following pages is the required information to help you accomplish these goals. You will learn the subtle differences that can take you to the plateau of being a consistent winning player with a necessary bankroll of just $1,500.

Introduction

Texas hold'em has many intricacies, and most of these will affect your play and your expectation in any game. If proper adjustments aren't made for the specific game you're in, you could suffer complications that you may not be expecting. You must make changes in your game to win at the optimal rate.

With a betting limit of $5, the casinos sometimes choose to hold a $2-$5 spread-limit game over a traditional $2-$4 fixed-limit game, or even the available $2.50 - $5.00 games that can be played. This gives the game several aspects of being one that will consistently draw customers. The limit to the number of raises can be up to five, which is above most games by one or two raises, while there is usually no limit to the number of raises if the pot is contested heads-up. On the surface, the skilled player would like the structure of the game from the perspective of being able to punish opponents who are playing too many hands and calling too frequently. While both of these points are valid, there are some more subtle differences that need to be taken into account to play the game optimally.

The goal of any gambler should be to maximize the expected win, while trying to minimize the standard deviation (or the amount any one-hour of play statistically differs from your expected hourly win). Unfortunately for winning card players, the two are not mutually exclusive. You must sometimes increase your standard deviation to increase your expected win, and vice-versa. If you have an adequate bankroll, you should usually play to maximize your hourly gain. You may find it easier on your psyche to play with a slightly smaller hourly gain with smaller fluctuations. This will give you more of a feeling of control of the game, and will also spare you from some of the "roller coaster" type feelings that can come from a game like this. I will point out both alternatives within the text of this book, so that you can choose the method of play you enjoy the most.

Many of the fundamental playing details of hold'em poker are not included in this book. You must be familiar with the rank of poker hands and basic rules of play. I have tried to address the specifics of the $2-$5 game in each playing aspect. You will want to study other texts on details of flop, turn, river play and game theory for Texas hold'em, while using this book to add subtle variations in your play to optimize your win rate.

Keep in mind that if you win 60% of your sessions, and your wins and losses aren't out of proportion to one another (generally your wins should be somewhat greater than your losses even in extreme cases), you will be a winning player with a respectable hourly gain. This means that you will lose 40% of the time! This margin is still quite good. Baseball teams that are at .600 and football teams that are 10-6 usually go to the playoffs! Consequently, your goal should be to win 60% or more of your sessions, and to work on winning the most money. The information that follows will help you do just that.

Games You'll Find

You'll find three basic games of $2-$5 hold'em and one offshoot $3-$5 limit game. The betting limits are similar but each game itself is slightly different and has an effect on your expectation as well as your standard deviation. These types of games are:

- Three raise limit, 10% rake up to $3.00, ($2-$5)
- Five raise limit, 10% rake up to $3.00, ($2-$5)
- Three raise limit, 10% rake up to $3.50 ($2-$5)
- Five raise limit, 10% rake up to $3.00, ($3-$5)

Most of the games have unlimited raising heads-up (just one other player). You must have started the betting round heads-up for this to apply.

The first type of game is the one that offers you the most stability, or the least volatility of the four structures. You can beat the game due to the horrendous errors your opponents will make. I should also mention that if you are in a game with opponents around your skill level, you'll lose money in the long run.

The five-raise game can be eruptive. You will sometimes find several *maniacs* at one of these tables, and your standard deviation can skyrocket. You need a larger bankroll (and patience) to play in one of these games. There are some players who will gladly play almost any two cards for $27 before the flop! This sometimes makes it correct to chase hands that you would routinely throw away *if you stay to see the flop*. If you have middle pair with an over-card and the pot is laying you 20-to-1 odds (i.e., there is $100 in the pot), it is often correct to call. If you find yourself in a game with a player of this type, you'll want to maintain your reputation as someone to be feared. That is, if you're going to play, make him pay for his mistakes. When you have K♦K♠, and you figure he's re-raising with garbage, encourage him to pay $27 to see the flop. Perhaps he will get lucky, but he will be giving you a great return on your money.

The odds are on your side, and if you have an adequate bankroll, you won't suffer in the long run, you'll gain.

Make sure that your starting hands, and succeeding calls are justified so that you're still playing winning poker (i.e., don't chase when you don't have a draw to a winning hand). In a game like this, I *never* get into a pot with trouble hands from any position if I think the pre-flop betting will go to five raises. These hands are: A-Q, A-J, A-10, K-Q, K-J, K-10, Q-J, Q-10 off-suit (of course, avoid **worse** hands). When the hand is suited, it is a different story *if* you're getting five other callers. I wouldn't recommend initiating the raises with these hands; you *will* make money on them by playing them conservatively before the flop.

I wouldn't even like to play Q-Q, or J-J for $27 if I knew about it ahead of time. You generally end up getting good enough odds to try for a 'set' (three of a kind) with these hands, that by the time you realize the betting will be capped (the maximum raises are taken), you need to stay. This is why the game is so volatile. While trouble hands have equity in normal games, they too frequently wind up making second best hands to risk money in pre-flop action. Certainly stay away from off-suit connectors (like 8♦7♣), and give yourself the best chance to make the *winning* hand.

The third game needs mentioning only because of the increased rake. The additional $0.50 per hand rake (which will often be collected) increases your hourly cost by $1.50-$2.50 per hour. Believe me. This can eat into your overall expectation. This is a substantial margin to overcome in a game where the biggest bet is $5. With solid play, in a favorable game, your costs can be reduced, and you can beat the rake. Some poker rooms also have a game with two blinds, one of $1, and one of $2. The play in the big blind is very similar to the play in a single blind game. The small blind, however is somewhat different in that I believe you should play almost any two cards for an additional $1. You can still throw away the ugliest hands. This is due to the tremendous implied odds on your initial bet that will immediately be laying you about 9-to-1.

The fourth game definitely needs special treatment concerning strategy. It is not a game I'm fond of for several reasons. The reputation of the game is one of "ram-jam" type poker where the pot is raised several times before the flop. It also has a reputation for building large pots, and it is the game that will give you the biggest fluctuations in your bankroll. You are likely to experience *large* swings in wins and losses.

Keep in mind that the correct strategy when playing in a large ante game is to play more hands. Hold'em is unique in that it generally only requires blinds and this necessitates different considerations. Due to the size of the pots, you will also be required (by pot odds) to chase after flops when you are behind. Notice that this is exactly what less skilled players in the game are doing. Therefore, the difference between your play and their play is less remarkable than it would ordinarily be. In the smaller ante game (with one $2 blind) you are not penalized for playing tight. You should still play tight in the $3-$5 game, but in a somewhat different fashion. (Note: With one $3 blind and one $5 blind, to call before the flop is $5.) You would be less inclined to get into a pot with small pairs or small suited connectors (like 7♣8♣) and would lean toward large suited connectors as your favorite hands. If the game is tight (most of these games aren't tight), you would prefer big pairs to the large connectors.

You must come in with a raise more frequently in the $3-$5 game because there is immediate value gained by limiting the competition in the fight for the $8 blinds. In the $2-$5 game, you can more frequently stick around with drawing type hands before the flop because it's only $2 to call. Your hands in the $3-$5 game require more immediate value, *and* staying power.

To summarize the general ideas in the $3-$5 game (which will not be covered specifically in this book, except that the required adjustments should be clearer after you've studied this text):

- You must be even more selective about the hands you play before the flop. (You will need to defend your blinds more often.)
- The looser play comes **after** the flop because of the bigger post-flop pots.
- Raise more frequently (if you're going to play) to $10 from most positions if you are the first one in the pot. If the hand is **Strong** ∞ or **Mediocre** you can occasionally just call (e.g., 9♠10♠).
- You can be more liberal (than you would in a $2-$5 game for $5) with wired pairs when you are in late position *if* you can enter the pot for just $5, and you're quite sure there won't be a raise.
- Closely watch pot odds by counting the number of bets in the pot at any given time.

For example:

If five players — including the blinds — have entered the pot for $10 (two bets), there are 10 bets in the pot. Thus, your first draw at the flop must be *at least* better than a 10-to-1 shot! While it's true that a flush-draw is 1.86-to-1 with two cards to come, you will likely have to call a bet on the turn (fourth card) as well. The financial return on your flush-draw is diminished by any following bets or raises. What type of draw *might* warrant a call? If you had A♠8♠, and the flop was Q♣8♥2♠ should you call (not considering possible raises)? There are three Aces and two 8's, that will make a strong hand, and two running spades will make a flush. You have five outs (cards that make a probable best hand) at ~ 4-to-1 or 20.4%, *plus* the 23-to-1 (or 4% chance) at the flush. I will neglect the small probability of making four 8's or 8's full of Aces for this calculation, but it works in your favor. This consideration is somewhat canceled out by the Queens than can fall and still beat the hand even if it does improve. You are left with a 3.1-to-1 chance at improving to a strong hand with two cards to come. You could then call a bet profitably if you figured you were up against someone with K♦Q♦! (You are truly a

3.06-to-1 underdog to this hand.)   Notice that you must compensate for an increased number of opponents in the pot when you make this type of calculation.

The other thing to always consider is the overall strength of the players in the game. Game selection will be the largest factor in determining your expected win rate in a game. You must evaluate the players in the game and decide just how frequent and which type of errors they are likely to make. Your income is directly related to the collective dollar value (probabilistically) of the erroneous calls (and less frequently, folds) the other players routinely execute. So make sure you choose your game wisely if you expect to make money.

General Considerations

Let's take a look at the way a standard situation compares in a low-limit fixed structure (e.g., $2-$4) game. A common practice in fixed-limit games is to bet with your good hands, such as four flushes and open-end straights. The effect of such a bet still gives excellent odds against a typical game even with a raise. For instance, in a low-limit game you might average five players before the flop in an un-raised pot. If you are in the pot with a flush-draw from an early position, and you bet, you might have two or three callers or you might face a raise. Well, your chances for getting a free card are almost non-existent from an early position anyway, but it only costs you a small bet to look at the turn. The implied odds are still well in your favor (the immediate odds from the pot are 10-to-1 with two callers and a raise). If you catch your flush, you will quickly profit due to the increase in size of the bet on the turn. You can see that if you have over-cards also, or even just one over-card that you figure to be good, you will show a nice profit in the long run.

When you are faced with the same situation in a non-standard spread-limit game ($2-$5), your odds are diminished greatly. For instance, if you have the same amount of callers and the same betting sequence after the flop (as above), your odds are reduced to immediate pot odds of 6-to-1 ($10 plus three $5 bets and a $10 raise is $35 minus the $3 rake or $32) to call the raise, with greatly diminished implied odds! While this makes the call correct, keep in mind that a good portion ($12) of the pot used to be your money!   Remember this when you call before the flop with suited connectors; it's much better to have position. Take a look at the players in the pot. Can you profit mathematically? If not, can you profit by playing deceptively? If not, you're better off not to play the hand.

You don't find many players in small limit games that fold on deceptive plays because:

1. If they are capable, they don't do it in small games because their typical opponents aren't usually making raises in a manner that makes it <u>better</u> to fold.

2. Weak players are going to call you if they think their hand is "pretty good" right to the river, almost without regard to what develops.

3. The players with some experience playing against deceptive opponents have discovered that the easiest way (not necessarily the best way) to foil them is to just call them to the river.

The more you confuse your weaker opponents, the more likely they are to call. Their thinking goes like this: "Does that Check-raise mean I'm beat, or that he's trying to get me to fold . . . I'd better call.

PRE-FLOP PLAY

Hand Selection

The play of the hands in $2-$5 spread-limit is at least as important as the play in a fixed-limit game if not more. The difference between the starting hand requirements is large enough that it probably involves some new thought processes on the player's part. I'm going to break the starting hands up into different *Types* of hands. You'll see that in general, the play of hands tends more toward "big card theory", but there is significant latitude depending on the type of game in which you are involved. The game you're in will greatly determine the type and number of hands you can play, and how you play them. The different considerations that we will look at are hands that:

- Play well vs. few opponents — $\varnothing$.
- Play well vs. many opponents — ∞.
- Play well with few or many opponents — ☏.
- Might play well or poorly vs. many or few opponents with **extreme** flop dependence — ☠.

Not all type hands that you will be playing, play *equally* well. Obviously a pair of Aces plays better than a pair of Jacks regardless of how many players are in the hand (in the long run). What I will try to instill, is an acute awareness of the number of players in the pot or who are likely to be in the pot, and what kind of hand is best to play given that knowledge.

When I say few opponents I mean four or less. When I say many, I mean five or more. Four opponents can sometimes play havoc with the return you are getting from the pot on your drawing hands, or likewise, give you more players than you'd like drawing at you with your big pairs.

If you've played the game quite a bit, you probably have a feel for what I'm about to describe. I'm going to detail exactly why you have these feelings. Whether you are an experienced player who enjoys playing few hands, or one who prefers getting into the fray, you will recognize what I'm saying just by the feeling you get from the hands I'll show you. (Please note that one of the biggest errors otherwise talented players make is to play too many hands.) The way in which I recommend playing starting hands may be different from how you have been playing them. While changing may be uncomfortable at first, the increased profits you will show should quickly get rid of your apprehension. Also, please be aware that the plays are not written in concrete.

I'm also going to attach a *strength value* to each hand. This will range from **Very Strong** to **Very Weak**, for each of the different *Types*. Sound confusing? Relax, this will become clear after you have heard the thoughts that accompany the recommendations.

The key is:

Very Strong	VS
Strong	S
Mediocre	M
Weak	W
Very Weak	VW
Few	$\varnothing$ (Mathematical symbol for 'null')
Many	∞ (Mathematical symbol for 'infinity')
Few or Many	☯ (Yin and yang)
Flop do or die!	♟

A hand that is VS☯ is "Very Strong versus Few or Many players"

A♠K♠ is an example of this type of hand. You will read in later chapters that this means that you want to manipulate the pot (make it larger) regardless of how many players are calling.

Because of the strength of the hand, you would be inclined to do what is necessary to get a lot of money in the pot before the flop. For instance, in early position, you might call the initial bet and re-raise the maximum if the pot's raised. If you aren't having any trouble getting callers, you can raise immediately. The thing to keep in mind with this hand is to discard it if you don't hit the flop (I will discuss this in more detail in the ☯ section). The $7 is already gone from your stack once you put it in the pot. If you bet or chase flops like

prepare to lose money in a <u>loose</u> game. In a <u>tight</u> game, you might be okay with this flop.

I will cover the play of all of the hands that you would consider playing. The concepts that I discuss for the Type of hands (∅,∞, ☯,♔), and how to play them before the flop, will follow, with a complete layout of the hands.

Hand Types And Categories Chart

⊘	∞	☯	☠
Very Strong A-A, K-K, Q-Q	**Very Strong** **A-10, J-10**	**Very Strong** **A-K, A-Q, K-Q**	**Very Strong** A-K
Strong J-J, 10-10, A-Q	**Strong** **Q-J, K-J, Q-10, K-10, 10-9, J-9, 9-8, 10-8, 8-7, 7-6**	**Strong** **A-J**	**Strong** 9-9, 8-8, **A-K**
Mediocre A-J	**Mediocre** J-10, 6-6, 5-5, 4-4, **Q-9, 6-5, 9-7, 8-6**	**Mediocre** K-Q	**Mediocre** 7-7, **K-K**
Weak A-10, Q-J, K-J, Q-10, K-10	**Weak** J-9, 10-9, 9-8, 8-7, 7-6, 3-3, 2-2, **Q-8, J-8, J-7, 10-7, 9-6, 8-5, 5-4,**	**Weak**	**Weak** A-9
Very Weak K-9	**Very Weak** Q-9, Q-8, J-8, 10-8, J-7, 9-7, 10-7, 9-6, 8-6, **8-5, 7-5, 6-4, 5-3, 4-3, 4-2, 3-2,** 7-5, 5-4	**Very Weak**	**Very Weak**

How To Use The Charts And Instructions

These categories provide principles on how to approach general playing conditions. You may find yourself in many games where the groupings can be altered *somewhat* to fit your exact situation. If you are just beginning in your attempt to beat this volatile $2-$5 game, you should limit yourself fairly strictly to the playing that I recommend. Recall that I've broken the hands into four different *Types,* based on how they *play.* I've also listed the hands *Categorically* in order of relative strength from <u>Very Strong</u> to <u>Very Weak</u>.

Some things may appear strange at first. For instance, you might question how the different categories relate to each other. I hope this is mostly straight forward. That is, obviously A♣K♣ is stronger in any instance than A♣10♣ (before the flop). What I'm trying to get across, is that you don't necessarily want to play heads-up against a tight player in a situation where he raised from an early position and you hold A♦10♦. Strong hands of any *Type* can usually stand a raise, and may often warrant initiating such a raise yourself, depending on position. The Weak *Category* of hands across the board requires special care, and usually you would like to see the flop cheaply. There are some exceptions to this rule that will be covered in the "How to play *Types*" sections. Also, keep in mind that the hands that I've listed as <u>Very Weak</u> of any *Type* should usually be played only in the blind ($2) or perhaps on the button with the appropriate number of callers and with _little_ chance for a raise from the blind. Remember you are looking for the flop to *hit you with a 2″ by 4″* before you put in any more chips.

How does a flop hit you with a 2″ by 4″? You're looking for a flopped two-pair, a straight or *open-ended* straight-draw using both cards, a flush or a flush-draw. There are some other exceptions, which I'll discuss.

Generally you want the best hand or a draw to the best hand, on the flop. If you have a good steal situation after the flop and you're in the blind, *take a shot*, and bet your hand. Make sure that you have a chance to win the pot on this bet, or that you have plenty of outs *and t*he flop looks as if nobody will particularly like it. It's important that you have a reputation as a player that *will show down a quality hand.* That is, the first idea that goes through someone's head when you bet out under the blind is that you *probably* have top pair and a strong kicker. You will play hands like A♣Q♥ (or even 10♦10♠) in the blind without a raise as well as the standard trash, if there aren't any raises. So, if you have

and the flop comes

your bet may win the pot against a few players.

Better players will raise you if they hold a Queen with a decent kicker (in which case you can fold), and weak players will call with all types of unlikely hands. A *call* from a better player on a hand like this will probably mean that he has something like Q-10 or Q-9 (or maybe even a 'set'). If you fear this situation, slow down (i.e., don't bet anymore) unless you hit your kicker. Most of the time if, on the turn, I check, and then a straightforward player bets, I'll give him credit for the better hand, and fold. Occasionally I might raise if I think he might be betting his Q-10, *and* that he will *fold* when I raise.

The weak player that just calls should be bet into until he raises.

If you stop betting, you are giving up too much value when he calls with something like 6♠7♣. Now, he may turn over a Q-10, but you'll make more money in the long run if you bet into him until you feel you're beat. (See the section on 'Calling Stations'.)

Let's see how to use the categories. Say you hold

from an early position. You just call the $2 (because it's S♣) and there are three callers behind you when the person right of the button raises to $7. You know that this player only raises with big pocket pairs, and I mean Jacks or better. The blind folds, and you feel pretty comfortable that the three previous callers will call a single raise, but may or may not call a double raise. It should be clear that you don't want to re-raise, because you are probably behind.

The question is, should you call at all? If you call the additional $5 and the other players call as expected, you will be getting greater than 6-to-1 on your $5. It's important that you can count on those three callers also calling a raise, otherwise your call is borderline or it's a mistake. You are looking for a 'set' on the flop, and must be wary if you do flop a 'set' and an over-card also flops (i.e., a Ten, Jack, Queen, King, or Ace). Notice, that if you flop a 'set', and play it fast when an over-card has flopped, someone with Aces wired will also be concerned that you have flopped a 'set'. Only when he flops *top* 'set' is he certain that he has you beaten, and he will usually display this by the fearlessness with which he re-raises you. If you suspect you are up against a bigger 'set', you can check and call to the river. I don't recommend dumping a middle 'set' at this limit unless you are against an *obvious* made flush or an *obvious* made straight with all five common cards showing.

Even in these cases, if you are heads-up, you will profit by calling one last $5 bet to make your opponent show you his hand. The reason this is profitable even if you are almost positive that he has you beaten, is that you do not want him to be able to make this play with impunity when he doesn't have a straight. That is, a deceptive player may make a play at you with two-pair when four flush cards or four to a straight are on the board. For this game, you don't lose money by calling here, because you will pick off enough plays to make it profitable. In addition, if you *do* fold a winner, it will cost you the whole pot.

What do you do with your same 9's when you're in early position and nobody else calls until the man to the right of the button raises? The blind folds, and you are left to either fold or play heads-up. Keep in mind your opponent. If he plays well and is observant (assuming you've played with him before) he will respect you entering the pot from an early position, and probably won't be trying to run over you (because you *might* hold A-K, or K-Q suited). There would be $11 in the pot at this point, and you are not getting the odds to hope for a 'set' on the flop. You might be inclined to re-raise here to clarify your opponent's hand. If he's not too skillful, he probably won't re-raise without good reason (i.e., A-A or K-K) although he might pop it one more time with A-K. Against an opponent that will play mind games with you before the flop, you're probably better off just calling, and resuming play after the flop. The reason is that you will greatly increase your fluctuations with this fast play, without increasing your expectation. In other words, you only want to play mind games if you're sure you can control your opponent.

What if you have put in the second raise, and your opponent re-raises allowing you to put him on one of the 'Big Two' pairs. Are you getting good enough odds from the pot to continue? Well, there is $31 in the pot, and you need to call $5 more. If you call you can expect pretty good action if the flop comes the way you want. In most games the rake is 10% up to $3, so you are really getting about 5.6-to-1 odds from the pot. You can most likely expect to win 3-5 bets ($15 to $25) if you hit your hand and your opponent misses his 'set'. This means you are getting implied odds of 8.6-to-1 up to about 10.6-to-1. This is really a borderline play! Remember, most of the money in the pot used to be in your stack. It will certainly reduce your fluctuations if you fold (maybe before you put in the second raise)! If you're like me, though, the game itself is enjoyable, and you *do* give the illusion of being an action player with this type of play. My advice would be, if you feel like *doing the tango*, then this isn't a bad place to do it.

PLAYING THE DIFFERENT HAND TYPES

The ∅ *Type Hand*

The hands in the <u>Very Strong</u> segment of this *Type* are the premium hands that everyone who plays the game relishes. They make your chips warm with anticipation. The top two pairs (A-A and K-K) are worth as much money as you can get into the pot before the flop; the only exception being if you have Kings, and you suspect anyone else to have Aces. When you realize this to be the case, you need to slow-down, and check and call. Very rarely do you need to fold Kings when you feel you are against wired Aces, because it just doesn't cost that much to make your opponents show you the hand. It is a different situation entirely if you suspect your opponent of having Aces, and an Ace flops! Now you are possibly beaten in any number of ways, and you can often safely ditch your hand.

Queens are usually worth a re-raise from a middle or late position because an early position raiser may have hands as weak as middle wired pairs and you would like to limit the competition. The question becomes, "What if the previous raiser re-raises"? As is often the case, this depends on your opponent. Let me give an example from a game. I was on the button with Q♠Q♣ and there were two callers in front of me. I raised $5. The blind (a selective player, but weak-tight) re-raised. You can imagine that this did not make me feel terrific, but I thought that he might be trying to isolate the hand to the two of us. In this game that didn't happen. The previous callers still called, and it was $5 to me with one raise left. I feared that the blind might have me drawing thin. I was pretty sure he had K's, or A-K. I got the *feeling* that he didn't have Aces by watching the manner in which he re-raised. I decided that I would charge the other two hands to be in the pot, and take advantage of my position versus the first player by re-raising. I'm not sure I can wholeheartedly recommend this play, because I was overplaying my Queens and this doesn't increase long-term winnings. This was a three-raise game, and in most cases against a tight player with other callers it would be better to just call and look at the flop. In a five-raise game a re-raise is a more volatile play that specifies your hand somewhat because if he comes back over the top (re-raises), you know that you need to flop a 'set'. Since I had capped the betting, I didn't need to fear a re-raise and I didn't gain information regarding the blind's hand either. So I thought, "If he has Kings, he'll most likely put me on at least one Ace, and this may give me a chance to steal if he folds his Kings on the flop when an Ace appears. If he has A-K, he'll be very likely to check and call with over-cards or bet if he pairs his Ace." Notice that if an Ace flopped and one of the other players lead, then my play was spoiled, and I would have most likely just folded. Neither of the other players would have made a play in that position.

The flop came J♠6♥6♦. Not really the flop I'd like because heaven only knows if this made one of the other two callers trips. The blind bet, and both previous callers . . . called. I got the feeling that the flop didn't help their hands. I raised to follow through with my play, representing Aces (the blind might also worry about a 'set' of Jacks). I should mention that if the blind re-raised I would need to fold, (See the *Some Difficult Plays* section). Well, the blind folded, begrudgingly, and I knew that he had Kings (because he told the person next to him). The turn brought a Queen, but the blind was still very upset that he'd been manipulated into folding his Kings (as well he should). This scenario is to demonstrate the strength of position *and* the importance of adjusting your play to fit the players in the hand. This player frequently just believed that he was beat. In hold'em, even though you may be trailing, position can overcome some obstacles against *some* players.

The Strong Category consists of some hands that are more profitably played differently than in a fixed-limit game. I almost always recommend to raise with the hands in the Very Strong Category to give you the best chance to win the most money. In the Strong Category, though, you can place yourself in an awkward position if you always raise with these hands. The hands are: A-Q, Jack's and Ten's. These hands are desirable, but need to be played with caution to ensure their profitability. Namely, it's very important to try to limit the competition at *some* stage of the hand, and not necessarily before the flop. The problem with the wired pairs (10's and J's) is that if you raise and get many callers, you encourage players to chase after the flop (and they usually don't need much prodding) with as little as an Ace or even minor over-cards like Q-J.

With A-Q unsuited, I rarely recommend to raise in early position. Raise in middle position if one or two weak players have entered for $2, otherwise just call. In late position, I'll usually raise against few players, and just call in a multi-way pot. I don't want to play this hand against seven players for $7, because I really won't have any re-draws even if I do catch a Queen. I will not initiate this kind of action. Depending on events, however, I may end up playing this hand for $7 anyway. The only straight-draw you can flop is a gut-shot (using both cards except a flop of 9-10-J), and this alone (even if it's correct to call due to pot odds) increases your fluctuations greatly. If you're in the blind, it's usually better to look at the flop rather than raising pre-flop with A-Q off-suit, unless you're playing against few players. You might often lead bet top pair or check-raise depending on the situation.

Back to Jack's and 10's. I recommend raising with these hands to limit the competition in early and middle positions. In late position, play them somewhat like A-Q with the exception that you can usually raise more liberally with Jacks. This is due to the fact that with 10's the extra over-cards (Jacks) that can fall will put you in a precarious situation that many more times. The strength of 10's is sometimes underestimated in flops with possible higher straight-draws. Keep in mind that no straight can be made without a 10 or a 5. So if you have two 10's, you've reduced the chance for players to make the higher straights against you. This doesn't come into play often, but it is worth mentioning.

If you don't like the flop when over-cards hit the board and you raised pre-flop, you should seriously consider folding your hand. If a player bets into you, with an Ace on the board, it may be a play by a deceptive opponent. *Do not just call this bet!* If you think a deceptive play has been made, *raise this bet.* Otherwise, fold. Your opponent can't be sure that you don't have the best kicker, (i. e. A-K), and if he doesn't fold, he'll certainly slow down without at least two-pair. If he calls, it means you are probably beaten by an Ace with a medium kicker — or better. Unless you improve, you should be through with your Jacks or Tens. Notice that this play is good for you to use in reverse. Let's say you have called from a middle position with 8♣8♦ before the flop, and the person to the right of the button raises, leaving you with no more than one other caller. If the flop comes something like A♣3♠7♦, it is often worth betting into the raiser. Notice that this may make him fold wired pairs that are better than yours. If you check, and he bets, you are in a guessing game. Against some opponents you could pull off this play with a check-raise, but an average player with a big, wired pair is likely to call you, and you've wasted $10. Try to get a *feel* for your opponent's strength.

The other hands of the ∅ *Type* are quite a bit weaker, and you should raise in steal situations, only. You should almost never call a raise with them, and don't play them from middle or early position without a very passive, loose crowd. If you never play these hands you probably won't cost yourself much money and you might reduce your fluctuations. However, you will twiddle your thumbs regularly. If you get bored enough to play a hand like one of these (e.g., K♣10♦) in a middle-early position (rarely), <u>don't</u> call a $5 raise that comes behind you. Just kiss the $2 in front of you good-bye. Wait for another hand and think, "I shouldn't have called the first $2." I've had many winning sessions without many of the premium pairs, and that is because the hands I *do* play, I play in a way that makes them profitable. Trouble hands (W∅), can be profitable in this game, but the easier you release them in times of danger, the more likely you are to make money with them.

The ∞ Type Hand

In a $2-$5 spread-limit game you will often find yourself with the latitude to play one of the hands of this type. Ideally you will want to get many players in on the flop, and subsequently on the turn. The idea being: You will get a flop that works well with your hand giving you a draw at the nuts, or otherwise a powerful hand. The most powerful hands of this type are the ones that will likely develop into a hand that will not be out drawn. That is why you find A-10 suited and J-10 suited at the top of the list. It may be worthwhile to note that all hands of the ☻ type could just as easily appear on the top of this list. In other words you will always be happier before the flop with an A♦K♦ than an A♦10♦! What the A-10 lacks is the kind of strength to be a strong hand heads up against a tight player.

There is kind of an interesting effect with this type of hand. Some authors are quick to point out that a hand being suited only adds a few percentage points to the value of the hand if you play showdown. That is to say, A-10 suited will win a five card hold'em showdown a few percent more often than A-10 off-suit. Let me preface this by saying that most studies that have been researched playing 'showdown' can be misleading if not almost irrelevant. That is, the play on the flop will far outweigh any handicapping based on all five cards being dealt, with no betting or raising. Also, keep in mind that fortunes are made on edges of 3%. This being said, heads up, A-10 suited is not very much stronger than A-10 off-suit. Against many players, though, it is much stronger. This is because the rank of your kicker can be paramount heads up, whereas against many players, the fact that you will be drawing to the nut flush (or straight) makes the big difference. (You will try to fold when out kicked.) You will also gain the additional equity of having back door flush-draws to accompany any other hand you flop, sometimes turning an easy fold into an easy call (or raise). It is important to realize that the flops you want to get with the ∞ type starting hands will generally be of the two-pair, flush-draw, and straight-draw variety.

If you consistently put pressure on your hand to win with top pair and kicker, you will be disappointed, regardless of the appeal of your starting hand in terms of overall strength. If you have Q♣10♣ and the board comes Q♦5♦8♠ you <u>may</u> have kicker trouble. Luckily, the game that you are playing in will usually have numerous players happy to play (to the river) with much worse kickers than your 10♣! If you are just called by a tight player, sometimes you will be shown a hand like K♥Q♠ after you've gone to the river.

As usual, it is important to note what your opponent's call or raise means. Hopefully, a decent player will realize that you are usually in the hand with a decent kicker yourself, and defer to your hand (by folding) when he has a weak kicker (although don't hold your breath for this to happen). When he has a kicker like a King, he <u>should</u> raise to charge drawing hands (diamonds or 6-7) a premium to draw. If he just calls, he will likely be just about where you are, and you gain a chance to outplay him if the board develops into something scary. You must be able to read your opponents well enough to recognize a scary card that probably didn't help anyone. Let me give an example. Suppose the board has developed as in the case above, (Q♦5♦8♠) and you are the first bettor among five players. These players include you, a tight player, one other very loose player, the blind and one other. If the pot was un-raised there would be around $10 in the pot before the flop. You lead bet, the tight player just calls, and the last caller is the loose player (everyone else folds). There is now $25 in the pot. Say the turn card is the 6♦. Well, this could be a scary card and surely could make a flush (the liberal caller may have made a straight)! Does this mean you should check? <u>NO!</u> I see this type of weak play all the time, and it costs players more than it ever saves.

If the loose player habitually bluffs, you might just check, and then leverage the board with a raise to get the tight player off a Q-J or another Q-10. The problem with checking is that you allow other players to bluff at the scary board. A liberal caller might be tempted to bluff on that board when you've shown weakness (checking the turn) not to mention that the tight player might seize the lead, and you'll probably have to fold.

If you bet out and you get two callers again, you're probably still all right. If someone has made the flush he will probably raise. The point is, even if the tight player isn't going to charge the other players to make draws, you should! Unless you know that you're in second place. The next card might be the 8♦ and the liberal caller could certainly have something that will beat both you and the tight player. He is unlikely to take a draw with a low diamond for $5 (assuming he doesn't have anything else). Maybe his hand is bad enough not to get a call at all. If you lose the liberal caller on the turn and the 8♦ does fall on the river, you might be able to get the tight player off a hand as strong as K♥Q♠! Believe me, even a tight player won't **just** call in this position with a K♦ or an A♦! In other words, if he raises, you can dump your hand. Remember, these players are trying to save bets (as you should).

It will be worth making this move (lead bet or raise occasionally) once decent players realize that you are playing strong hands with prudent overall play, and that you ordinarily have what you are representing. Even liberal callers will usually note that you seem to be turning over strong hands consistently. According to game theory you should be bluffing with a frequency that makes it equally probable for you to have a winning hand compared to the chances you are bluffing as the ratio the pot odds are offering your opponent if he calls your bet (i.e., a pot of $50 would warrant a *random* bluff 1 out of 10 times). Of course, this must be adjusted to the player whom you're against depending on how often he can be expected to call. Your image will take care of itself with solid play, which is why strong players will allow you to steal a hand in this type of situation (occasionally).

So how do you play hands of this type? The stronger the hand, the more willing you should be to put additional bets into the pot before the flop. The hands in the Very Strong category can stand two or even three bets in multi-way pots. The Strong category hands can usually only stand one raise *after* you have already called $2 with several other players. I don't recommend calling a raise cold with one of these hands. You may commit yourself to the hand for many more bets and this can be expensive if you run into a bigger flush. In addition, you will find yourself forced to take long shot draws in marginal situations due to the large pot size. Constantly monitor your odds after the flop taking into account backdoor possibilities. You should be more inclined to *induce* increased pre-flop betting the later your position, and the higher the probability of many callers. Keep in mind that just because you raised, you don't have to bet on the flop unless you like it.

An example of play might be — in an un-raised pot, you have J♠10♠ in early position and the flop comes 8♦7♣2♠. If there is the typical $12 in the pot and someone bets after you've checked (you should only rarely semi-bluff in this position) and two players call, with the last action to you, what should you do? There is now $27 in the pot and there are four 9's that give you the nuts. A Jack or a 10 may make your hand best, but it may also kill you. Keep in mind, the more loosely your opponent plays, the less likely it is that he has exactly the two cards that make the best hand at any given time. This is because the likelihood of him holding 9-10 or J-9 as opposed to all the other garbage he plays would be smaller than a player that plays only quality hands.

Don't take this concept too far, though. Some players are way too loose before the flop, but have a good idea about where they are after the flop and won't necessarily call without reason.

Back to the initial discussion. If you are up against two-pair already, neither your Jack nor your 10 will be any good. Likely betting or calling hands might include; A-8, A-7, or A-2; 8-7, 5-6 or 9-10; and let's not forget the fact that any 'set' will *at least* call. Notice, too, that someone might call with one pair and *any* over-card as a kicker. Where does this leave you? First of all, a semi-bluff raise should be quickly dismissed as a play. These players aren't going to fold for one bet, and you might be re-raised, costing you money. You have a draw that will make the best possible hand, and some other opportunities for improvement as well.

An A-8 would surely bet, and it is a hand that your J♠10♠ has 10 outs against for an easy call. Notice that your play in a $2-$5 game would be different in a late position from your play in a fixed-limit game. In the $2-$5, you would be less likely to try to buy a free card with a raise on the flop (because the bet is the same on the flop as it is on the turn).

Generally speaking, the fact that many weak hands will call, and that you are likely to get action if you make your hand, a call is usually in order. If you suspect that an opponent holds 8-7, you shouldn't usually call. The way I would ordinarily play the hand in this situation, is to check and call on the flop, and possibly bet out or check-raise on the turn, depending on the turn. If I hit either my Jack or my 10, I will probably bet, but if I pick up a spade that doesn't affect my straight-draw (even if it's a K♠) I *might* check-raise. I now have 12 (perhaps more) outs that normally would win the pot for me, and I might get a hand like J♣8♣ out (which is good). The idea behind betting out when my lesser preferred J, or 10 falls, is to find out if I have over-paired the previous lead bettor. If he has a 'set', straight, or two-pair he should raise, but he probably will just call (or perhaps he might fold) if he can no longer beat my top pair. If any 9 falls on the turn, I'll also bet out, because it will give me the most action, and I might even get three bets in if the original bettor raises. A check-raise in this position is usually a weaker play in terms of money making ability, because the callers are making a big enough mistake by calling the $5, and you will probably get plenty of callers. You will make more money in the long run if you lead bet.

The ☻ Type Hand

This is the smallest *type* in terms of number of hands that belong to it. You will be glad you got the hands though because they are as "blue chip" as poker hands get. The worst players make money on these hands, and you are going to make more, much more. You can raise with any of the hands in the <u>Very Strong</u> Category from any position. You won't necessarily want to do this as a habit because you can throw in any number of deceptions with any of these hands. If you're in a game where almost everyone that was going to call $2 will call $7, then you will get abundant action regardless of your position, and you can raise at will. If you are in a game where players will fold, respecting the power of your early position raise, sometimes it's better to call $2 and hopefully get to re-raise a raiser that acts one or two positions to your left. One thing that I don't recommend is to make the bet $5. The reason is: To keep sharp players from putting you on a drawing hand, you will have to raise with other hands to $5 (like medium pairs). You will still need to raise to $7 on your big hands, because players sometimes feel that a $5 bet is an invitation to a family pot that promises to grow quite large. Again, I feel that you are giving away too much about the make-up of your hand with a $5 bet. I recommend always raising to $7 to reveal nothing — unless you're playing short-handed.

These hands are strong enough to play against many opponents, and if you get only one other caller (or raiser) you can still be in good shape. (You can see the section on Ace-King to get some insight into how the suited variation plays more powerfully than the off-suit hand.) **A-Q** and **A-J** play similarly to the **A-K** with the exception that if you are against other big hands, the kicker will be important. You will be in a better position to decide the importance after the flop comes. Obviously, no one will have a better flush-draw than you do in *your* suit (with the negligible exception of a straight flush), and it will become obvious if that will be a determining factor on the flop. If you don't catch your flush-draw with **A-Q**, or **A-J**, you would prefer to have top pair with an Ace kicker, than a pair of Aces. That smaller kicker can still cause you trouble with tight players.

Even though **K-Q** is in the <u>Very Strong</u> Category, it requires some special attention. You will occasionally find yourself in a pot with other big hands against you. The reason **K-Q** ranks as <u>VS</u> is that it has additional ways of making a straight. If you are against Aces, A-Q, or A-K suited or not, you may have problems, and spend quite a bit of money determining just exactly how much trouble you have! You still love those flush-draws, but if you get much action after the flush hits the board you are very likely against the nuts.

My tendency with these hands, is to try to get money in the pot before the flop with whatever artistry is required. One good thing about most games of the $2-$5 limit is that players will find many reasons to call after the flop. So if you try a creative pot building maneuver in early position (i.e., trying to re-raise a middle position raiser), and the betting round ends at the $2 level, you will likely get plenty of action after the flop even if you flop a hand as big as two-pair. Please note that you will have two *BIG* pair and have little to fear from over-cards except for straight-draws. Ideally, you would like to be dealt these hands on or near the button. Since many players raise with marginal raising hands in this game (contrasted with players that are entering from all positions with *strong* hands for just $2), your opponents will often assume that you are raising just to take advantage of your button. Well, you are taking advantage, but not in the way they think. Rarely will *anyone* fold (except the blind) when you raise on your button.

The advice that it is a bad habit to 'check to the raiser' seems to be widely known now, because it seems harder and harder to get a free card on the flop with a raise before the flop. You will still get opportunities to take a free card, and often I recommend doing so if your hand doesn't hit the flop, unless you feel you can win the hand immediately (maybe against a few players who you think don't like the flop either). Keep in mind, that someone may be lying in the weeds, dying to check-raise you with some monster hand (or worse, try to take you on the milk route). If either of these situations seem probable, don't bet your over-cards.

You are likely to win large pots with these hands, but you will also have to invest in some flops that turn out to be just abysmal. This most often happens when the flop comes with many suited cards, but none of them match yours. Get rid of the hand, unless otherwise compelled.

The only remaining hand of the ☙ type is K-Q off-suit. This is a hand that many players incorrectly evaluate as to its strength in a given situation. While it can be fairly strong short-handed, it is only more powerful than hands that aren't very strong. It generally can't stand too much pressure in pre-flop raises because the type of hands that generate substantial action in other players tend to be big favorites against K-Q. If you are going to put the hand under some stress pre-flop, you must have good control of any opponents against whom you are contesting the pot. If you choose to raise in situations where few players have limped into the pot, keep in mind that you need to pair on the flop or readily be able to bet and take the pot. You should usually avoid playing to your over-cards unless you are against few, weak opponents who would bet or call with hands like 8♦7♥ on a board like 2♦8♣5♠.

The hand plays well versus many opponents when it is only $2 to see the flop and you pair one of your big cards. If the texture of the flop is such that there aren't any likely draws, you can usually take the money down with a bet. In addition, you will often be called when you have your opponents badly out-kicked when you have top pair. It also plays well when you flop an open-ended straight draw. Sometimes if you pair either of your cards you will have over-paired your opponent who has a hand like J♦7♠. A compelling reason why you don't want to play hands like J♦7♠.

The ☠ *Type Hand*

This is one of my favorite *Types* of hands to play, because when you win you usually drag a fairly decent pot, and the hands are easy to discard if you don't get a flop you like. This isn't *always* the case with the paired hands of this *Type*. For the other hands, *if you play correctly*, you will find a <u>*Type*</u> of hand that is full of reward, and not high on risk.

An entire section is devoted to the play of A-K, so I will refer you there for insight into profitable play of this hand.

The <u>Strong</u> category of the ☠ *Type* of hand is composed of middle wired pairs — 8's and 9's — and A-x suited (where x is any card 9 or less). The pairs are of a rank such that it is relatively infrequent that you will see a flop without over-cards. This means that you frequently need to rely on a 'set' to have a powerful hand. If you are heads-up against a player with something like Q♥10♥ before the flop, you are a small favorite. Notice by holding either one of these pairs you interfere with his chances to make a straight. You can make it very expensive for a person to continue playing if neither a 10 nor a Queen come on the flop. What also happens, with 8's and 9's, and to a lesser extent, 7's, is that you may not have top pair, but if no one has matched the over-card you will have the best hand. This happens infrequently in a "family" pot (where many players are in), but with only two-three other callers, you can usually bet as if you have the best hand — because you usually do. Players will let you know if you are beaten with a call or a raise (depending on your opponents' style). However, you will get many calls from players with a pair other than top pair that are lower than yours. Note: It is important to pay sharp attention to the cards that fall on the turn and the river, because you must be aware if your opponent has made two-pair. It is worthless to try to track this with players who'll play "any two" for the obvious reasons.

Say, for instance, you have 8♦8♠, and the flop comes J♣5♥2♠

in an un-raised flop. You bet and get one caller (who would usually raise holding a Jack with a good kicker). If he doesn't have a jack with a weak kicker, with what other hands might he just call? He might peel off a card (with or without proper odds) with 5♠6♠, A-5, K-5 of Clubs or Spades and A-2, K-2 of Hearts or Clubs. Notice that in this case, even if he is playing 3♦4♦, you don't have any *additional* turn cards to fear. A player will often let you know when he hits his card. Look for the tell tale signs like a bet or a raise. If one of these scare-cards falls on the turn, look for signs that your opponent would check-raise you. You may want to check behind him and then call on the river (you may pick off a bluff). If you are out of position and the turn card doesn't help any of the above possible draws, by all means bet again (unless you feel that your opponent does hold a Jack with a weak kicker). Even if the Ace or King falls, you are usually better off betting than waiting to see if your opponent bets. He may fear the over-card too, and get rid of his hand.

We can put the **A-x** hands and the **K-x** hands together in *style* of play but not strength. They play very much the same, but the Ace makes your hand substantially stronger in play than the King. The Ace is superior when four cards come to your flush, when you have top pair and your Ace or King is your kicker, or when Ace high wins the hand. The reason these hands fit into the ♣ *Type* is because of their strength against a hand like **J-10** suited in a short-handed pot. They also play well against a big field because if you make your flush, *or* two-pair, you have a *big* hand. You get substantial value when you flop two-pair because an opponent will take much longer to figure out that his Queen kicker to his Ace or King is no good.

If you hit your big card, you have a problem. Your top pair may be best but you could easily be out-kicked. It is usually worth a bet to try to take the pot right there against a few players, but you don't want to get any more involved than that one bet (usually). An exception would be when you are in position with something like A♦7♦, and an opponent lead bets. If he might let go of a kicker up to a 10, then pop it. I should say that there are very few players that will do this, so be very selective with this play. If the board is such that you have back-door draws, you can be somewhat more liberal with a raise. For instance, if the board comes A♣6♦5♠, giving you three to a flush and three to a straight, you would be more likely to make this raise. This is true specifically when you won't ordinarily have to call a bet on the turn, giving you a chance to decide if another bet is in order, or to take the free card. I must reiterate, that there must be some chance that your opponent will fold for this play to make money.

Every hand in this *Type* is excellent to use to re-steal what you suspect to be a "steal" raise (from a late position opponent) when you're in the blind. Blinds are generally stolen less in this game than in a fixed-limit game. What you are more likely to run into is, when someone with a decent hand, upon everyone else folding, decides to end the hand with a $7 bet to take the $2 Blind. His idea is to proceed with the next hand (and gain $2 in the process). When you re-raise with any of these hands (♟), you will usually surprise the fellow who raised (or woman, though men make this play more often in $2-$5). Your opponent may fold right then. If he calls, your follow up bet on the flop with *most* flops will (amazingly) often win you the pot.

While others may recommend just calling the initial raise — and you do put yourself more at risk by raising — you will re-steal often enough in this situation to *more* than make up for the times you are clobbered by a bigger hand. The funny part is: If you mistakenly get involved against something like Q♣Q♠, you can still win if the flop hits your hand!

Ace-King Revisited

The subject of many heated discussions at the Poker Table (regardless of the limit) is how to correctly play A-K. Often the suited cousin of this same hand becomes lumped into the same discussion and the same playing style. Many players don't make as much money on either of these two hands as they should, (Note: There are 12 off-suit A-K's and only four suited A-K's), and they are different in subtle, but significant ways.

Let's talk about the off-suit version of this powerful hand. Yes, I said powerful. It is simply a strong hand that usually makes the *best* hand when you hit the flop. It rarely makes a second best hand. Added to this, it is the best hand that isn't a wired pair before the flop. The reason players lose money on this hand (in the long run) is that they become excessively attached to it. Usually it is worth three bets before the flop, but if it completely misses, it may be valueless. To make my point stronger, if you don't hit the flop, you *may* have a worthless hand if someone hits the flop. This is paramount in a typical $2-$5 spread game because players will stick around with their A♠7♠ if they pair their 7 on the flop. This leaves you drawing to a King. It's rarely correct to draw to one over-card, and you wouldn't even know if a King was good, because your optimistic opponent might have K♣7♣!

A-K off-suit made the (VS♣) category in my hand-rating chart because it gives you a variety of playing choices before the flop depending on your position and what you expect your opponents will do. Keep in mind that the fact that you hold your A-K makes it less likely that you are facing a wired pair of either Kings, or Aces (although this does happen). When you run into substantial action before the flop, you will find yourself often up against J-J or Q-Q. You may even be facing Ace-Big Kicker (including another A-K). In a typical pot though, you will probably have the best hand before the flop.

It is in your interest to limit the competition with this hand **when you are in the pot with more than a call pre-flop**. Notice that I've implied that there are times when you are better off just calling before the flop. These times might include when you are in early position, specifically if the players in later positions tend to raise with medium strength hands. You then have the intention of re-raising.

You might also just check in the blind with an off-suit A-K with the intention of check-raising on the flop (even if you have just two over-cards). Otherwise, it might be in your best interest to make it three raises if someone re-raises you (when you are in a middle or late position). Keep in mind that you would much prefer to have position on the person you are re-raising, but you may want to retain control of the hand even without position if you are heads-up.

This is because the thinking — assuming that your opponent is one of the thinking types — that your opponent goes through, is along the lines of: "Now, he re-raised, that means he probably has Aces or at least Kings wired or maybe he has A-K." If he has J-J or Q-Q (or even Kings), he is likely to just call, and if he has A-A, or A-K, he might raise one more time. If the flop then comes rags, he will probably bet into you, if he's not timid, in which case you can usually get a free card with a raise. If he is timid he will check and call with most wired pairs or worse hands like Q-J. Against a timid player it's usually safe to check to the river (if you don't hit your A-K), and show down the hand.

One weakness inherent in not raising before the flop is that it will make your opponents' hands somewhat more difficult to read. Because you have entered for just a call, your opponent will not know the high quality of your kicker if you make top pair (this same problem applies when not raising with big pairs). Therefore, he will not be able to distinguish your post-flop raise from one that represents top pair, a 'set', or two-pair. If he has two smaller pair he will frequently just call to the river. If you bet on to the end, you may be betting for value with the second best hand, and this can sometimes cost you a bet (where you might have otherwise checked).

If your opponent is one with good playing skills, he might correctly read your raise as one that indicates a strong kicker, but other players won't. This can make the precise play of your hand a little more difficult than if you had played the hand aggressively the whole way.

After major pre-flop raising, there will be a substantial amount of money in the pot, and unless you run into three or four players, you have some control over the action after the flop. If you don't hit your hand, you may end up going to the river with just your A-K (you may be getting correct pot odds to call with these over-cards). This _doesn't_ mean that you have to bet and try to make other players believe you are playing a big pair. This is what costs most players money with this hand. Many players in the $2-$5 game will go to the river with a wired pair as weak as 10-10 regardless of over-cards or pre-flop action. Not only that, but if you run into a player who is apt to play something like Q♥5♥ for $2 up to $27 and he pairs his 5, he may call to the river with that pair of 5's on the chance that you are holding exactly A-K.

You are probably not in danger of giving free cards against a weak player, and if you need to check to the river, then do so. Take this approach: You are happy to play the hand for a substantial investment before the flop, but you will release the hand or not put it under _undo_ pressure if you don't catch on the flop. With this in mind you will find — if you keep track — that you are profiting on A-K, and are happy to hold it in your mitts.

What about the suited version of the same hand? This hand has strength and the flexibility to adapt to many situations. It plays well against many players or few players. In addition, it can sometimes show down a winner on it's own without any help. Ace-King suited usually gives you more than one way to win, with possible straights, flushes, and big pairs with the best kicker.

The reason this hand has so much flexibility is the extra value you get when you have over-cards to a straight or a backdoor flush-draw. Some poker books have said that this only increases your chances of winning a hand with a flush by a few percentage points, and this is true. The *play* of the hand becomes more affected by this extra *out* because of the value it adds to the drawing chances you have. Let's look at an example:

Suppose you have A♣K♣ and the flop comes K♦7♣9♦. In analyzing the flop, you know that nobody has made a flush or a straight *yet*. Substantial action from another player could come from a player holding: Two-pair, a 'set', or maybe something like K-Q. You won't know how it affects your hand when the board pairs (other than the King), but you will know that your hand has improved if the next card is the 4♣! The odds are funny in this situation. The chance of two running clubs is ~ 23-to-1. However, once the *second* club has fallen, your chance of getting the flush on the river is back to the standard 4.11-to-1. If you were up against an opponent with K♥7♥, you have more ways of winning than if you held A-K off-suit. This difference gives you *many* wins over time that would have been losses, and you get this advantage by merely having the cards suited.

Some Difficult Plays

Let's talk about some of the more difficult plays in the $2-$5 game. It is imperative to try to control the size of the pot and the number of players to maximize your chances of winning any given hand.

Occasions will arise when you are in a game against a player who has studied Hold'em and is making plays that are effective in fixed-limit games (e.g., $3-$6). This type of play includes an occasional raise on the button with hands like 9♣8♣ or 7♥7♠. Often you will see him enter the pot with a "straight" $5 bet. When this happens and you have entered a pot in early position with something like A♦Q♣ — or maybe you're in the blind with the same Ace-Queen — you really don't want to play it against the whole table. Even though you may not like it, you should usually re-raise. This play, hopefully, will isolate the hand to you and the raiser, or at least to hands that you should be able to read. If you walked into a legitimate raising hand like J♥J♦, you still aren't that much of an underdog and you can actively control the amount of action after the flop.

Notice that you have a different situation if the raise is from an early position or if the raise is from a player that makes it $5 with (mostly) power hands (e.g., K♣K♥, or A♣K♣) as well as other hands. You may be better off folding rather than even calling the $3 additional dollars against a large number of players.

Now suppose you're in the same situation with a trickier hand like A♥x♥. You really need to try to get a feel for the type of raise the late position player is making. Is it a steal raise? Or a raise to increase the size of the pot? Or is it a raise with a power hand? If the raise is to $7, it should be fairly easy to pass, since there will be stronger places for your money. If the raise is to $5, you need to consider the number of other callers you will get if you call. Notice that if you re-raise and limit the field (maybe), you will be in an awkward situation when your Ace falls on the flop and the other player who bet $5, has something like A♠J♠.

The play I prefer is to call <u>fast</u> (as if it's an obvious position raise) with many previous callers and hope they all call behind you — or just fold. The flop you want is for two hearts to come, (two-pair would also be nice) or perhaps top pair (not Aces) and a backdoor flush-draw. Note, that if you have <u>two</u> cards to a gut-shot straight with a backdoor flush you can play the hand if the action isn't heavy *and* if you are getting the right pot odds. For example, you hold

And the flop comes

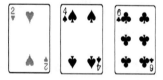

By the way, when I mean play, I don't mean checking and calling. I mean possibly check-raising, or betting on a semi-bluff. If you don't catch on the turn, and the players who called on the flop are likely to call again, you are essentially finished with the hand. (See the section on Special Drawing Situations for more on this subject.)

Let's look at some of the smaller pairs and medium suited connectors (M∞). When you are in a game that is loose and passive, you can call with many of these hands in middle position.

Be careful if the person on the button frequently raises to $7, because you just don't have the equity in one of these hands to play for $7. It's much better to pass.

In considering your pot odds, you should count the before-the-flop pot in terms of big bets. That is, if there are six callers, there are only two $5 bets in the pot! ($12 minus the implied $2 rake is $10 or two $5 bets). You can see now why you have to catch very solid on the flop! You can check-raise less also, because players are making mistakes by calling in many situations when you bet. You sometimes can't even call with a flush-draw heads-up in an un-raised pot without at least one <u>good</u> over-card. Though you might raise — with position — against a player who would fold middle pairs or top pair with a weak kicker.

Your ability to know what you are up against can save you money. The following type of play occurs rarely, but when it does occur, recognizing this situation will make you two to three bets richer than the average player.

You are dealt Q♦Q♠ from a middle position and raise. You are re-raised by a player that would normally call with A-K (suited or not) and will only re-raise with big wired pairs down to Jacks, and he does just this. Regardless of how many other players are in the pot with you, if the flop comes J♣4♠7♠ (Jack high at any rate), you are probably beaten. The best possible scenario is that he also has Queens. Well, this doesn't happen very often! You are probably beaten because even if he doesn't have an over-pair, he has a 'set' of Jacks. Certainly slow down. If it's heads up you might consider folding against the simplest opponents. The opponent must not be very deceptive *and* you must be able to predict his hand *for certain* not being A-K or other big cards. Also, remember to check your pot odds. If there is $150 in the pot, it would be worth pulling off *at least* one card. Notice that you can apply this theory regardless of the size of your pair.

If you hold

And raise before the flop, which comes:

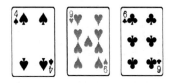

If you are fairly certain that your prudent opponent has a wired pair and you lead bet, if he can call or raise you are probably beat. In fixed limit games, a player will frequently raise with over-cards on a flop like this. This play is less frequently made in a typical $2-$5 game.

Another situation that arises is when you are playing heads-up against an opponent who will raise with hands like K♣Q♦ and A♦J♠ from almost any position. If you call a raise with a hand like A♠Q♠ and the flop comes rags, your aggressive opponent may continue to bet the hand as if he has a big wired pair. Notice that you don't know for certain that he doesn't have a big wired pair, but he might also have Ace-King, which would win in a show down. This is a very difficult situation to gauge, but if you are going to call to the river, you should usually put in a raise at some point in the hand. Notice that a player who raises with K♣Q♦ will probably call a raise to draw to over-cards when he holds A♣K♥. Therefore, it may be better to wait until the river to raise his bet if you hope to make him fold his hand.

PLAYING INSTRUCTIONS FOR EACH PLAYABLE HAND

Adjusting Your Play Of Starting Cards

The flashcards (pp. 53-68) recommend a style of play that will be effective even against a table of good players. There is quite a bit of deception and aggressive play suggested prior to the flop. You must make adjustments to these recommendations depending on the game's personality and sometimes even based on the table's perception of you as a player. If you strictly follow the suggested play it will be a profitable way to play starting cards. However, you are not an automaton, and probably will not be able to play an entirely emotionally detached, scripted game (nor would you want to). You must adjust to your sense of the game in a positive manner. Your *goal* is to play optimally, and part of your dynamic, high percentage approach is to adjust when necessary to the players and the game. This is just *one way* out of many, to play starting cards. Certainly, vary your game. If you find yourself often playing hands that aren't on these flashcards, you're playing too many hands to win the most money possible.

More often than not, you will find yourself in a loose, passive game, which is good. However, when players find plenty of reasons to gamble after the flop, it becomes less valuable to risk money prior to the flop with questionable hands. Remember, many of the raising situations prior to the flop are designed to eliminate your competition. If raising doesn't have that effect in your game, then it may actually cost you money! For instance, if you raise in early position when holding Jacks, and hands like K♦9♠ or A♣10♥ don't fold, then part of what you trying to accomplish is failing. If you are against an entire table of players like this, it may be a disadvantage to create a larger pre-flop pot. You are probably in big trouble if over-cards hit, and you won't usually be getting good enough odds to try to get another Jack.

Also, if the game is wild, sometimes it is in your interest to keep the betting less lively with flop vulnerable types of hands — ∅ {**Strong** or weaker}, and ♞{Any}. Remember, any time that pot size makes the bad players and the good players play alike, your fluctuations will increase without noticeably making your expectation higher.

The other reason to make alterations in the way you play starting hands is if you are facing opponents who often enter pots with strong hands without raising. If an opponent is selective about his hands and yet doesn't ever raise, even with A-K, Aces, Kings or Queens, you must pay special attention each hand that he plays. This should not keep you from playing your premium hands aggressively, but you may have to forego some of your more aggressive plays with marginal hands if he is also in the hand. Otherwise, you might fall into re-raising traps with a weaker hand. If he sees you show down a mediocre hand that you raised with (like A♦J♠), he may start to re-raise with his stronger holdings. Certainly tighten up on your starting requirements if there are several opponents who are tight in your game, and just stay away from weaker hands altogether. (Steal after the flop somewhat more frequently.)

Another time it is prudent to tighten up your play is if you have been losing. Much of your success will depend somewhat on the respect that other players give your bets and raises. If you have been losing, you should severely limit your aggressive play with hands that are not superior. It is also better to reduce your semi-bluffs and other such tricky plays more than normal. This has to do with the fact that if you have been losing, your opponents are liable to feel as if **they have control over you**! They will feel empowered to manipulate you in ways that they have previously only fantasized. Keep in mind that if you run badly for three hours, and yet play with prudence, you should ordinarily be able to recoup your losses with 15 minutes of winning hands.

Don't become carried away in the opposite regard. You can play a few more of the marginal hands if you have been winning **and** have good control over your table. Steer away from trying to

establish 'heaters' with ridiculous hands. It's a sure way to throw away several of your hard earned bets.

Another time you may want to vary your play on the side of being more aggressive is when you have been playing tight, and your opponents feel confident that when you raise you have a big, wired pair. More players will try to run you down if they feel that they know where you are at in a starting hand. You must throw a deceptive pre-flop raise with hands like 7♠5♠ occasionally, to keep them guessing. In fact, adding one suited hand to those with which you raise adds a good mix to your game. This adds one hand that you will raise with that should randomize your game. You can change this hand every session making your raising hands more difficult to read. I don't recommend that your suited hand of the day contain a ten. The ten is an important card in many playable hands and you will frequently get into difficult spots with any single ten, why pay more for the trouble?

Keep in mind that these flashcards contain one, *specific* guide, but the concepts behind what appears on the cards are the most important things to grasp. As your playing experience grows, you will know the proper time to deviate from the recommended plays.

In summary, use the following flashcards as a basis for establishing a winning, basic starting hand strategy, and then use the rest of the book to make the appropriate adjustments according to the players in each hand of each game.

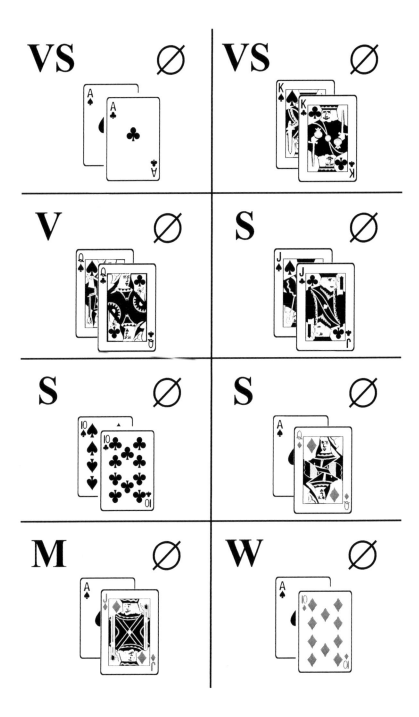

K♠K♣

Early	Middle
Raise	**Raise**

Late	Button
Raise	**Raise**

Blind

Raise or Check-Raise Flop v. Many

A♠A♣

Early	Middle
Raise	**Raise**

Late	Button
Raise	**Raise**

Blind

Raise or Check-Raise Flop v. Many

J♠J♣

Early	Middle
Raise	**Raise**

Late	Button
Raise	Raise/Call v. Many

Blind

Check-Raise Flop V. Many/Raise

Q♠Q♣

Early	Middle
Raise	**Raise**

Late	Button
Raise	**Raise**

Blind

Check-Raise Flop v. Many

A♠Q♦

Early	Middle
Call/Raise v. Raise	**Call/Raise**

Late	Button
Often Raise	**Raise**

Blind

Check-Raise Flop/Re-raise

10♠10♣

Early	Middle
Raise	**Raise**

Late	Button
Raise	Raise/Call v. Many

Blind

Check-Raise Flop v. Many

A♠10♦

Early	Middle
Fold	**Call**

Late	Button
Call	**Call**

Blind

Check/Fold v. Raise

A♠J♦

Early	Middle
Call/Fold v. Raise	**Call**

Late	Button
Call/Occ. Raise	Call/Occ. Raise

Blind

Check/Fold v. Raise

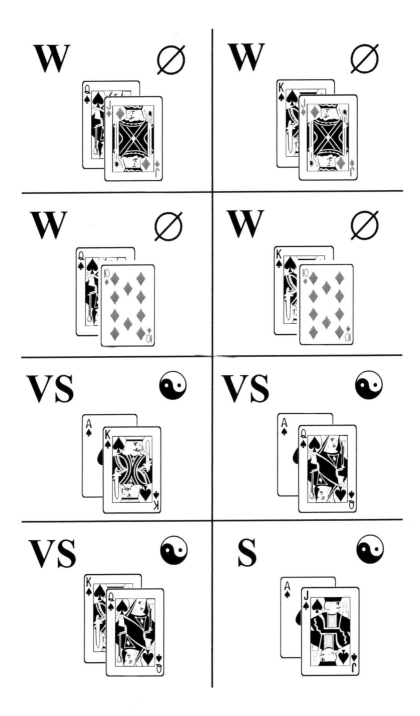

K♠J♦

Early	Middle
Fold	**Fold**

Late	Button
Call	Rarely Raise v. Few

Blind
Check/Fold v. Raise

Q♠J♦

Early	Middle
Fold	**Fold**

Late	Button
Call	Rarely Raise v. Few

Blind
Check/Fold v. Raise

K♠10♦

Early	Middle
Fold	**Fold**

Late	Button
Call	Rarely Raise v. Few

Blind
Check/Fold v. Raise

Q♠10♦

Early	Middle
Fold	**Fold**

Late	Button
Call	**Call**

Blind
Check/Fold v. Raise

A♠Q♠

Early	Middle
Call—Re-Raise	**Call/Raise**

Late	Button
Raise	**Raise**

Blind
Sometimes Raise/Call v. Raise

A♠K♠

Early	Middle
Call—Re-Raise	**Call/Raise**

Late	Button
Raise	**Raise**

Blind
Usually Raise-Call/Raise v. Raise

A♠J♠

Early	Middle
Call—Re-Raise	**Call/Raise**

Late	Button
Call/Raise	**Often Raise**

Blind
Sometimes Raise/Call v. Raise

K♠Q♠

Early	Middle
Call—Re-Raise	**Call/Raise**

Late	Button
Call/Raise	**Often Raise**

Blind
Sometimes Raise/Call v. Raise

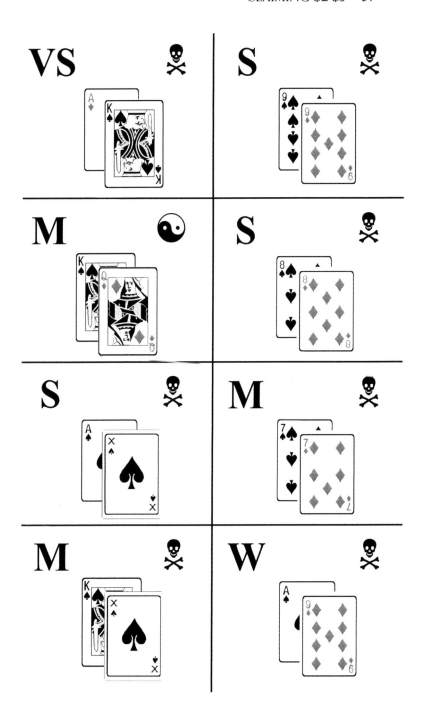

9♠ 9♦

Early	Middle
Call/Occ. Re-raise late raise	Call/Occ. Re-raise late raise
Late	**Button**
Sometimes Raise	Raise v. Few/Call

Blind
Usually check/Occ. Re-Raise

A♦ K♠

Early	Middle
Raise/Call	**Raise/Call**
Late	**Button**
Raise	Raise

Blind
Raise—Check-raise flop v. Many

8♠ 8♦

Early	Middle
Call/Occ. Re-raise late raise	Call/Occ. Re-raise late raise
Late	**Button**
Sometimes Raise	Raise v. Few/Call

Blind
Usually check/Occ. Re-Raise

K♠ Q♦

Early	Middle
Call/Fold-wild game	**Call**
Late	**Button**
Raise v. Few	**Call v. Many**

Blind
Check—Call v. Steal Raise

7♠ 7♦

Early	Middle
Call	**Call**
Late	**Button**
Call	**Call**

Blind
Check—Call v. Steal Raise

A♠ x♠

Early	Middle
Call	**Call**
Late	**Button**
Call	**Call**

Blind
Check—Call v. Steal Raise

A♠ 9♦

Early	Middle
Fold	**Fold**
Late	**Button**
Call	Call v. Weak Players

Blind
Check-Fold v. Real Raise

K♠ x♠

Early	Middle
Fold	**Call**
Late	**Button**
Call	**Call**

Blind
Check-Call v. Steal raise

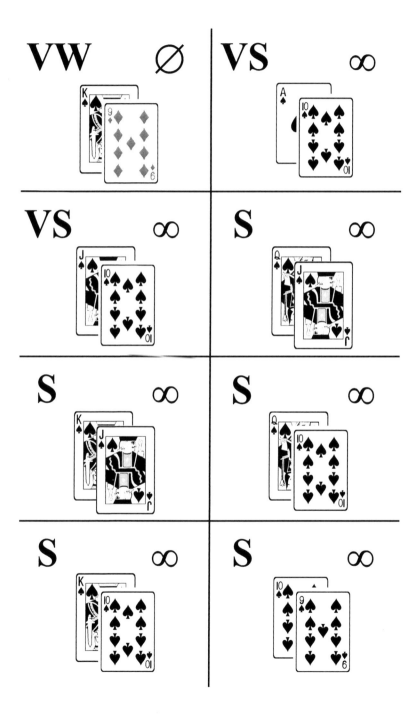

A♠10♠

Early	Middle
Call	Call

Late	Button
Call	Rarely Raise

Blind

Check-Sometimes Raise

K♠9♦

Early	Middle
Fold	Fold

Late	Button
Fold	Call v. Weak Players

Blind

Check/Fold v. Real Raise

Q♠J♠

Early	Middle
Call	Call

Late	Button
Call	Rarely Raise

Blind

Occ. Raise—Call raise v. Many

J♠10♠

Early	Middle
Call	Call

Late	Button
Call	Rarely Raise

Blind

Occ. Raise—Call raise v. Many

Q♠10♠

Early	Middle
Call	Call

Late	Button
Call	Rarely Raise

Blind

Occ. Raise—Call raise v. Many

K♠J♠

Early	Middle
Call	Call

Late	Button
Call	Rarely Raise

Blind

Occ. Raise—Call raise v. Many

10♠9♠

Early	Middle
Call—Fold v. Raise	Call

Late	Button
Call	Call

Blind

Occ. Raise—Call raise v. Many

K♠10♠

Early	Middle
Call	Call

Late	Button
Call	Call

Blind

Check-Call v. Steal raise

9♠8♠

Early	Middle
Call	Call

Late	Button
Call	Call

Blind

Check

J♠9♠

Early	Middle
Call	Call

Late	Button
Call	Usually Call

Blind

Rarely Raise

8♠7♠

Early	Middle
Call	Call

Late	Button
Call	Call

Blind

Check

10♠8♠

Early	Middle
Call	Call

Late	Button
Call	Call

Blind

Rarely Raise

J♠10♦

Early	Middle
Call-passive game	Call

Late	Button
Call	Call

Blind

Check

7♠6♠

Early	Middle
Call	Call

Late	Button
Call	Call

Blind

Check

5♠5♦

Early	Middle
Call/Fold v. Raise	Call

Late	Button
Call/Fold v. Raise	Call

Blind

Check-Call v. Steal Raise

6♠6♦

Early	Middle
Call/Fold v. Raise	Call

Late	Button
Call/Fold v. Raise	Call

Blind

Check-Call v. Steal Raise

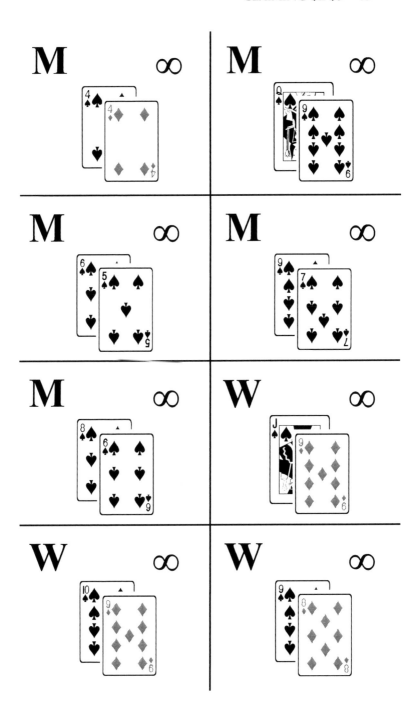

Q♠9♠

Early	Middle
Call-passive game	**Call**
Late	**Button**
Call	Call
	Blind
	Check

4♠4♦

Early	Middle
Call-passive game	**Call**
Late	**Button**
Call	**Call**
	Blind
	Check

9♠7♠

Early	Middle
Fold	**Fold**
Late	**Button**
Call v. many	**Call**
	Blind
	Check

6♠5♠

Early	Middle
Call-passive game	**Call**
Late	**Button**
Call	**Call**
	Blind
	Check

J♠9♦

Early	Middle
Fold	**Fold**
Late	**Button**
Fold	**Call v. many**
	Blind
	Check

8♠6♠

Early	Middle
Call-passive game	**Call**
Late	**Button**
Call v. many	**Call**
	Blind
	Check

9♠8♦

Early	Middle
Fold	**Fold**
Late	**Button**
Fold	**Call v. many**
	Blind
	Check

10♠9♦

Early	Middle
Fold	**Fold**
Late	**Button**
Call v. many	**Call v. many**
	Blind
	Check

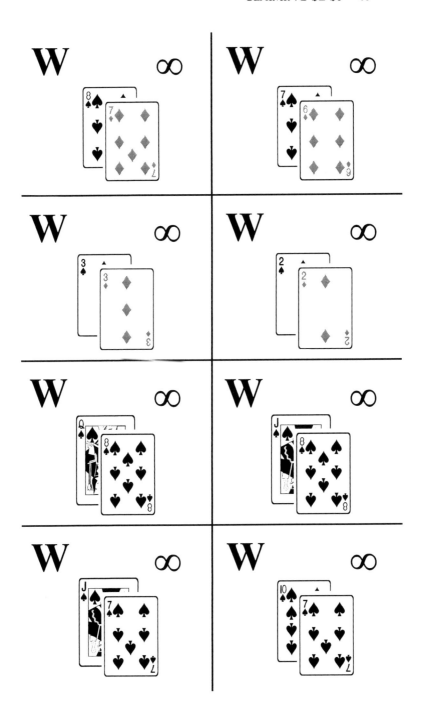

7♠6♦

Early	Middle
Fold	Fold
Late	Button
Fold	Fold
	Blind
	Check

8♠7♦

Early	Middle
Fold	Fold
Late	Button
Fold	Fold
	Blind
	Check

2♠2♦

Early	Middle
Call-passive game	Call
Late	Button
Call	Call
	Blind
	Check

3♠3♦

Early	Middle
Call-passive game	Call
Late	Button
Call	Call
	Blind
	Check

J♠8♠

Early	Middle
Fold	Fold
Late	Button
Call-passive game	Call
	Blind
	Check

Q♠8♠

Early	Middle
Fold	Fold
Late	Button
Call-passive game	Call
	Blind
	Check

10♠7♠

Early	Middle
Fold	Fold
Late	Button
Call-passive game	Call
	Blind
	Check

J♠7♠

Early	Middle
Fold	Fold
Late	Button
Call-passive game	Call
	Blind
	Check

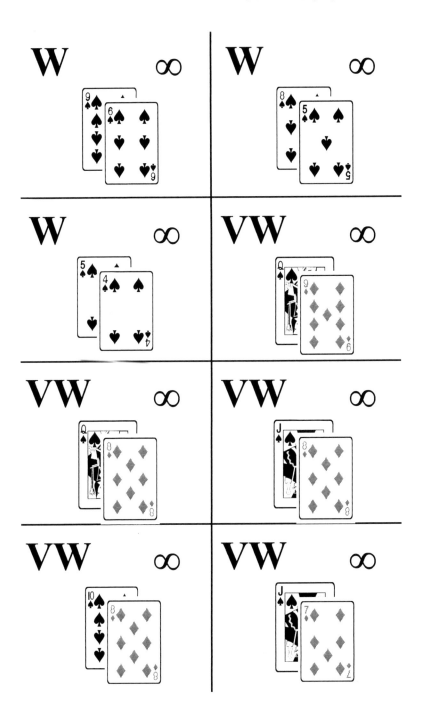

8♠5♠

Early	Middle
Fold	Fold

Late	Button
Fold	Call v. Weak Players

Blind
Check

9♠6♠

Early	Middle
Fold	Fold

Late	Button
Call	Call v. Weak Players

Blind
Check

Q♠9♦

Early	Middle
Fold	Fold

Late	Button
Fold	Call v. Weak Players

Blind
Check

5♠4♠

Early	Middle
Fold	Fold-Rarely raise

Late	Button
Fold	Call v. Weak Players

Blind
Check

J♠8♦

Early	Middle
Fold	Fold

Late	Button
Fold	Call v. Weak Players

Blind
Check

Q♠8♦

Early	Middle
Fold	Fold

Late	Button
Fold	Call v. Weak Players

Blind
Check

J♠7♦

Early	Middle
Fold	Fold

Late	Button
Fold	Fold

Blind
Check

10♠8♦

Early	Middle
Fold	Fold

Late	Button
Fold	Fold

Blind
Check

POST-FLOP PLAY

They'll Play To Beat Aces

An idea that should save some frustration versus poor to mediocre players: Even players with a very loose requirement for opening hands will notice if you play tight and aggressive. They will notice that your starting requirements are very rigid, and may accuse you of playing only "Aces, Kings, and Ace-King" especially if you've raised before the flop. Now, while you know this isn't true, and that you have been folding other hands that didn't develop, (like wired under-pairs,), your opponents won't be able to determine necessarily what your hand is, but they will start to play to beat <u>better</u> hands.

So, if you're in a game with some experienced, not necessarily skillful players, and you raise from early or middle position, they will play to beat Aces wired. Now you may not hold Aces, but they are going to play or draw to <u>beat</u> Aces. You probably won't run into any raises from an unsophisticated player until he has Aces beat. Let's say you raise with Q♦Q♠ in middle position, getting a couple of callers, and the flop comes with under cards. If one of these players raises, you are most likely looking at **two-pair**. This same player will most likely slow-play a 'set' or better on the flop (whether it warrants it or not). The good news is, that when you re-raise one of these players, you will slow down his betting because he usually figures you for a better hand than the one you have. That is, if you re-raise with these same Queens, he might figure you for a 'set', not an over-pair (I'm sure you can see his lack of logic). This may allow you to get free cards in an attempt to out-draw the smaller two-pair **if** pot odds warrant such a play. Understand that if the board pairs, you won't necessarily know if your opponent has filled up, but his level of confidence in betting should tell you. Also, if you do get substantial action from a weak, calling player, he probably has you beaten badly, and you can usually dump your hand.

A 'Set' In $2-$5

There are several things to consider in the play of a 'set' in the $2-$5 betting limit that you'll encounter. One consideration is the way you think about the small and medium pairs you hold before the flop. You can be somewhat more liberal playing wired pairs from different positions in the game if it's full of players who will not raise very often. You must be more careful if there is significant raising going on before the flop.

Let's take a look at the difference in the dynamics between a fixed-limit game and a spread-limit game. If you were playing in a $2-$4 fixed-limit game, you would consider calling with a smaller pair (e.g., 4♦4♥) if you could get five other callers for the initial $2 bet. This would give you correct odds to make money if you flop a 'set'. The play of this holding ranges from check-raising the flop to betting the flop and check-raising the turn in order to extricate the most money from your opponents without giving them any free cards. Don't slow-play yourself out of the pot! The chances of flopping a 'set' or better are around 7.5-to-1 giving you enough action after the flop to make a profit if there are at least five callers.

In the $2-$5 spread game, remember that the bet after the flop is immediately $5 (usually). What does this do to the number of callers you need before the flop? It reduces it *if* you can indeed see the flop for $2. In a fixed-limit game, if you flop a 'set', bet and get three callers (with five callers before the flop) you will have probably gained $16 for your initial bet of $2 (8-to-1 up to this point in the hand). In a $2-$5, if you get three callers after the flop, you have gained $25 to this point (assuming you have the best hand). This is a realized gain of 12.5-to-1! You can reduce the number of callers that you need before the flop, and also loosen up on your position requirements because of this mathematical effect.

Using the same reasoning, because the initial $2 bet can be raised by $5 before the flop, you will drastically reduce the odds you get on your same small or medium pair because of the small (relatively) post flop bet. In other words, if you were to call a $2 bet in a $2-$4 fixed-limit game, and then the pot was raised from a late position with five other callers, you would be getting good enough odds to warrant another call. Remember, the *second* $2 will be giving you odds of 11-to-1. In the spread-limit game, your second call would be giving you odds of 7-to-1 if everyone called (which they may or may not do depending on the game). If you flop a 'set' in the spread-limit game, your immediate gain (assuming you have the best hand) would be reduced to 6.7-to-1 on your original $7. Less than the 7.5-to-1 return you would like.

Depending on the qualities of the game you're playing in, (loose or tight) you may still be correct to call the second raise, but your realized gain will be less than that you will experience in a fixed-limit game of similar size. You may find yourself in a situation where you have made a play with negative expectation. Notice that the realized gains apply to any fixed-limit game when referred to in odds. This play — calling the second raise — will also raise your fluctuations because you are basically playing "long shots" even if they are positive gain opportunities.

The important thing to keep in mind is that your position is extremely important in this situation (you hold 4♦4♥). You will have less knowledge about what other players' actions will be if you call in an early or middle position with small or medium pairs. In addition to this, you will not know how many players will call a raise from a late position player, and this could put you in a losing situation. If you consider these factors, you should be able to gauge the additional (or reduced) opportunities for playing the small to medium wired pairs.

The question then arises as to how to play the 'set' that you have flopped. Generally, in the $2-$5 game, you can just bet your hand, almost without regard to position. The reasoning is, you increase your chances to make it three bets if someone with top pair (or two-pair) raises, and you don't risk giving any free cards. On occasion you might want to check-raise many opponents from an early position because you will be doing this occasionally with other holdings, like a four-flush or top pair. In other words, you are adding variety to your game to confuse your opponents. Also remember that if someone who is not a maniac gives you substantial action and there is no possible straight or flush, you must beware that he has a bigger 'set'. I recommend paying your opponent off to the river to make him show you his hand.

Whatever tack you choose to take with your hands needs to be supported with other plays that will reinforce the desired response from your opponents.

Get Out If You're Behind

One of the most frequent errors that players in the $2-$5 game make is calling when they are overwhelming underdogs against the hand that they believe their opponent to have. Let me give an example. If a player, who you know will raise with an Ace with a *reasonable* (at least 10 or bigger) kicker, raises your bet when you have something like A♦5♦ and the flop has come A♥8♠K♣, you need to fold your hand, almost always. The reason is that you are a 7-to-1 underdog to pair your 5♦, (given that your opponent hasn't already made two-pair). Notice that your opponent will improve just as often as you will and you will lose when you both improve. In other words, he will hit his kicker with the same frequency as you will, and he'll almost always win.

It's important to point out the quality of this flop that makes it easy to fold. A good player will not call a bet, let alone raise with *any* draw in an un-raised pot (because there really isn't much of a draw possible). Some players would occasionally semi-bluff raise with Q-10, being the aggressive players at your table. If you fold in these situations, you will reduce your standard deviation without making a losing play. You will have better places to punish an opponent for being too aggressive. Of course, if the opponent is out of line, you may have to pay him off.

Notice that you are in a different situation altogether if you have a good kicker. If you hold A♦Q♣, and you are raised (with the same flop, A♥8♠K♣), even if you fear you are against exactly A-8, then you have more ways to win than in the previous example. Not only can your Queen give you the best hand, but if another King comes you will also have the best hand — against that opponent. You have a 3-to-1 chance to improve (not including a running over-pair to the 8's) and your opponent has an 11-to-1 chance of catching another 8 in two cards (in which case you're in trouble). If your opponent held K-8, you would even be better off. Of course, if your opponent might hold A-K, then you should be very careful even if you do hit your Queen. I'd be tempted to check and call to the river, rather than give any additional action. A player that will play any Ace regardless of the kicker will hit two-pair with Aces more often than other players, just because of the greater number of hands they're playing that contain an Ace.

The way the betting might go is: I'm in middle position, and there is no raise before the flop. Again, the flop is A♥8♠K♣. I bet with my A♦Q♣, and am raised by the 'any ace' player. It becomes heads up and I re-raise. If he is **not** an <u>aggressive</u> player and raises again, I can safely put him on A-K or a 'set' (probably of 8's) and dump my hand. Note: I would not usually re-raise against a very aggressive player, because: (1) I might be re-raised when he has two-pair, (2) I can't buy another card (like I might against a more timid opponent), and (3) I won't necessarily gain information as to whether he has a 'set' enabling me to fold. Therefore, I would just check and call to the river (because he might have something like A♣J♦).

Another situation in which weak players make expensive mistakes is when they flop middle or bottom pair with a kicker under the top card on the board. Unless the pot is laying wonderful odds, it is much better to fold. If the flop comes A♠8♣K♥, an early position player bets and you hold K♦Q♦ — you should probably fold. The situation is different if you are against a possible steal bet from a late position player. Notice also that if you are going to play, you must usually raise. Someone might be on a steal if it was checked around and the player right of the button bets. If everyone folds before the action gets back to you (in middle position) then you could raise. If a Queen, Jack or Ten hits on the turn, proceed with caution, because J-10, Q-10, and Q-J are the types of hands with which tricky players would try to steal on a semi-bluff. . In addition, if an opponent is a solid player, this card may give him two-pair with his Ace. Usually, players will not bet a pair of eight's from an early or middle position because they fear someone with a pair of Kings or Aces will call or raise behind them. The exact same theories apply when you hold a wired pair that upon the flop becomes lower than top pair. If you held 9's and the flop were to come A♠8♣K♥, you would be fairly certain that you were beat once there was a bet or a call. In other words, if anyone can bet or call on the flop shown, you are probably beaten and would be drawing very thin to your 9's (11-to-1 with two cards to come). If you were in late position after the flop, with the 9's, you might be better off taking a free card and seeing what happens than betting. You are likely to be called by a weak player with a better hand even if the other player would be making a questionable call with a hand like K-10. Of course, if you have only two weak-tight opponents who have both checked, a bet should win the pot. So evaluate the situation and take advantage of your late position.

To summarize: When you look at a flop like the one in the example, seriously consider folding if you don't have what figures to be the best hand. You won't have profitable chances of drawing to anything.   (Which is exactly why it's a good flop for you when you hold A-Q).

All Gut-Shots Are Not Created Equal

You are going to flop many inside straight-draws in hold'em. Choosing the proper plays in these situations is essential to your success as a $2-$5 player. Common word of mouth advice recommends never drawing to this type of hand. This is misleading and can be harmful to your bankroll.

One of the reasons that hands like medium two or three gap suited connectors are undesirable to play before the flop is that one of the *better* flops that you can hope for is a gut-shot. This can be beneficial if you also get a flush-draw, or a back door flush-draw, but on it's own merits, usually it's a weak hand.

So what qualities make a gut-shot a desirable hand? Simply put, it is over-cards and/or back-door flush opportunities. It is essential that you are drawing correctly according to the money in the pot, whether you think just one or both of your over-cards is good, in addition to what typically would be a four card out with your inside straight.

In the $2-$5 game, you should limit your over-card drawing attempts with a gut-shot to strong over-cards. These should usually be K-Q, A-Q, A-J, and A-K. You hope to be good if you catch either of your cards. There are exceptions to this rule, and they are usually dependent upon the pre-flop activity. For example, if six players limp in before the flop, and you're in late position with J♠10♠. The flop comes 7♠8♦2♥. If the blind bets and you get one other caller you can usually at least call. Of course, a raise may be a better play if there is a chance that either or both of your opponents will fold. If you are against a bet heads-up or a hand that you feel is Ace-top pair at best, a raise can be profitable if your opponent might fold. In small pots it's often best to fold.

One of the most frequent occurrences of a strong gut-shot

straight-draw is when you hold Ace-King and the flop comes with two other cards needed to make Broadway (Ace high straight). While this can be a good flop for your hand, if you are getting callers after the flop, be careful when the turn card pairs you, but could give someone else a straight. This can be a difficult hand to play because the same player may have two-pair. This is one of the times where the hand becomes much easier to play with few opponents. Unfortunately, you are more likely to get decent odds to look at the turn card with more players involved in the hand. Keep in mind, that the only time a player won't be concerned about the strength of your hand is when he holds the nuts! In other words, if he only holds two-pair, he is likely to have the same concerns about your hand, as you do about his. Therefore, if a player bets out, when you pair your Ace on the turn (drawing to a flop like Q♥10♣3♦), and you raise, a player with a straight in this situation will almost always re-raise. Depending on your opponent and the amount of money in the pot, you may not want to lead bet. Free over-cards are no longer really a danger to you, and you may have a worse hand than your opponent, so it may be preferable to try to finish the hand as cheaply as possible.

TURN PLAY

How Much Should You Protect Your Hands?

There are many times in a typical game when you will wonder whether it is appropriate to raise or even re-raise a pot after you have flopped a hand that you like. The way you handle these situations will greatly determine how large your fluctuations are, and will also affect your expectation. This is the area in your play where you will be trying to squeeze every possible dollar out of an advantageous situation. Often the quality that separates similarly skilled players is their ability to distinguish situations in which they truly have an advantage. This level of skill requires practice, introspection, as well as theorizing over specific plays that you and your opponents have made.

The better you become at these skills, the more frequently your plays might appear strange to lesser skilled opponents. For instance, if you have A♥5♥, a flop comes A♣7♠2♦, and you raise when a prudent opponent lead bets out of the blind. Your opponent shows down A♠10♦ after calling your raise — and it's checked to the river. Several things have happened. Most players will wonder why you raised with such a weak hand. Your reason will be specific; you raise because **he** knows that if you hold Ace-Big Kicker you will want to force other hands out with what is probably the best hand. Also, you feel that your opponent might bet some hands other than top pair, and you **may** have the best hand. The strongest reason for your raise, however, is to give your opponent a chance to fold when he holds Ace and a random, hopefully small kicker. Against an opponent who would not fold **any** Ace, or only bet a strong kicker you would not raise and certainly, you should usually fold.

Another time you may have to put more bets into a pot than most players would, is when the actions of previous players — whom you know well — lead you to believe that your hand is best even though it's not that strong. An example might be, when you hold

A♥J♥. The flop comes A♦K♦6♥, and a player who almost always bets drawing hands and isn't selective about the suited hands he plays, lead bets. Another aggressive player, (familiar with the lead bettor) who usually raises pre-flop with A-Q or A-K (this time everyone just limped in) raises. You should make it three bets (assuming no other callers). Most of your opponents (including those not in the hand) will think you have a 'set'. Ordinarily you would play a 'set' that way. Instead you have strongly played a specific hand against particular opponents whom you know very well. If you have misread the situation, you will appear **maniacal** to your opponents. You must count on more action from them when you raise in subsequent hands. Remember, confused opponents tend to call rather than fold.

How about when you flop a hand that is either probably the best or the nuts, and a card comes on the turn that may make your hand second best? This might occur when you flop a 'set', or a straight and a third flush card comes on the turn. In the case of having a 'set', regardless of whether your opponent really has a flush or not, you are almost always getting good enough odds to call in case you improve on the river. If you feel your opponent is semi-bluffing with one card (e.g., the Ace) of the flush suit, (and maybe a pair or better) then you might raise. Most opponents won't take this aggressive stance without a made hand, especially after you've shown great strength on the flop. You don't ordinarily have to pay off the bettor on the river unless the pot is large or your opponent is tricky.

In the case of the straight, you must base your decision on the opponent, the board, and the power that you demonstrated on the flop. The flop is Q♦8♦9♣, and you put in three bets on the flop with J-10. When the 2♦ comes on the turn, and a very predictable opponent bets into you, you can almost always fold your hand if you don't have a J♦ (you may still want to fold depending on the opponent).

Another example: You hold 7♠8♠ and bet from middle position

when the flop comes 5♦6♣9♦. If the turn card is Q♦, and an aggressive opponent who would draw to over-cards raises when you bet, you may want to at least call. He may have just made a pair of Queens with a diamond draw. Sometimes it's even better to re-raise in this situation. If your opponent doesn't have a flush, your second raise may cause another opponent to fold a hand like 8♣10♣. If your first reasonable opponent puts in a third raise, you can safely fold. Notice that this play may cost you an additional bet, but you may mistakenly cost yourself the whole pot if you fold, or if you just call and a Jack comes on the river.

The case can also be made for playing somewhat less aggressively than you might ordinarily play. For instance, if you hold A♦K♥, and the flop comes 10♦J♥K♠. When a tough opponent lead bets, you may or may not want to raise. First of all, if another player calls your raise, you are in trouble. If he doesn't have two-pair he may be <u>even </u>stronger. Secondly, if your opponent has flopped a straight, you will get more action than your hand can stand (meaning you'll presumably need to fold). Therefore, you may be better off just calling (assuming the pot is large enough to refrain from folding). This will allow you to fold cheaply if someone raises behind you, but will increase your return on the hand if it **is** the best (he might have lead bet with a hand like A♠J♦). He might even continue to bet to the river in which case he's betting your hand.

Special Drawing Situations

One important thing to remember when you are playing poker in a $2-$5 game is that many of **your** opponents have no idea what would be the right play even if they knew **exactly** what cards their opponents held. This is to say, in many situations if you turned your cards face up in the middle of the hand, you would find several players at your table who would not know the correct play! This is great for you — one convincing reason that the game is profitable.

There are other times when it is difficult for anyone to know what the proper play would be. This occurs frequently in multi-way pots. It would be beyond the capacity of most players to calculate the profitability of certain plays based on the mathematics alone. Even if they had time to try it. This section will cover a few of these situations so that you are prepared when they arise.

There was an article in *CARD PLAYER* magazine regarding just this type of situation. The author held wired Kings, and was **sure** one of his opponents held Aces. There were 19 bets in the pot, and another King flashed when it hit the muck before he had called the last bet. Even the author, a very experienced player, was not sure of the correct play. It turns out, there was enough money in the pot to continue to try to flop a 'set'! Believe me though, that the calculations for determining this are not something a person can accomplish before the action gets to him while sitting at the table!

Generally, the draws that you will be making decisions about are not as uncommon or peculiar as the above example. There are some that occur frequently, so that if you skillfully read another player's hand, you should be in the position to take advantage of your knowledge with proper strategy. In doing these calculations away from the table, you will attain immediate knowledge of the proper mathematical play. While some skill is required to calculate the proper odds correctly, it is beyond the scope of this book to teach the proper probability calculations. There is excellent literature available if you desire to learn. I recommend Sklansky's <u>Getting the Best of It.</u>

What I will do is provide some of the more common confusing examples, and give you an idea of what the correct payoff needs to be from the pot to warrant taking your draws.

One common scenario is when you flop a gut-shot straight with a back door flush-draw. The back door flush-draw adds the mathematical equivalent of one out to your draw with two cards to come. So you are slightly less than a 4-to-1 underdog after the flop. The calculation on the turn is straight forward. Either you have 12 outs (2.6-to-1) or four outs (10.5-to-1) depending on whether the turn card is one of your suit.

Another tough spot is when you have top pair with a big kicker, and you feel that someone else has two-pair. This brings up two possible predicaments: One, where your opponent has two smaller pair, and two, where he shares your top pair with a smaller second pair. It may be impossible to distinguish between these two situations, not to mention those where your opponent has made a 'set'. You are bound to make mistakes, but the following information should help you make the most prudent decisions.

First, when you are against two smaller pair. You can hit either of your cards on the turn or river. Let's look at the math. You have five outs on the flop (3.9-to-1) and eight outs on the turn (4.75-to-1). You should adjust upward from these figures for the times you are wrong and your opponent makes a full house. How does this work? There are two ways to look at it: (1) How much will it cost? (2) How often will he make a full house? If you take a conservative stance when the board pairs, it will probably only cost you an extra $5 (when you call the bet on the river), so you can adjust the size of the required pot by this much. Your opponent will make a full house 16.5% of the time (with two cards to come), so if you plan to play aggressively, you may prefer to use this percentage figure. You should be able to get a feel in the event your opponent fills up when one of the flop cards is paired.

The other circumstance is when you have top pair and a strong kicker, and your opponent has two-pair, but you both have top pair. For instance you have A♦K♠, and the flop is A♣6♥2♠. Strong play from an opponent will indicate at least two-pair, but maybe a 'set'. Of course, sometimes it is impossible to know which it is. Notice that if the top pair were Jacks instead, with the rest of the flop remaining the same (i.e. J♣6♥2♠), you should be more inclined to give your opponent credit for the 'set'. Since many players play **A-x** suited (not to mention any A-x off-suit), this situation will occur repeatedly with Aces. It will also be difficult to tell when your opponent has made a full house (even assuming he really does start out with just two-pair). If the board pairs, your opponent could have made a full house or could have been counterfeited. You must watch your opponent closely to try to read him for clues.

Apart from these reading and playing skills, let's look at the math again. If your opponent has top and bottom pair, you have six outs on the flop (3.14-to-1) plus the small chance of a running pair larger than your opponent's second pair. On the turn you may have nine outs (4.11-to-1). If your opponent has the top two-pair, you only have three outs on the flop (7-to-1) and unless the turn card is higher than the second highest card on the flop, you still only have three outs (14.33-to-1). So, if it is likely that you are against the top two-pair, it is usually prudent to fold. The same adjustments should be made to the odds in the pot as in the first example ($5 or 16.5%). The exception being that you may want to increase your requirements for the size of the pot by an additional two bets for those occasions when your opponent has a 'set' and you are drawing to two running cards (something you would prefer to avoid).

Another common drawing situation is when you have a wired over-pair to the flop and you suspect that your opponent has two-pair. Notice that this is similar to the example where you have top pair, with the exception that you have fewer outs with a wired pair. You only have five outs (3.91-to-1) on the flop, and it may be tough to distinguish which card on the board will help you if it pairs. The other problem with a flop that yields an advanced player two-pair, is that other players still in the pot have a bigger chance of having a straight-draw. It is for this reason it is to your advantage to have a wired over-pair that interferes with these opponents' opportunity to make a straight. This would happen if you held 10♠10♥, and the flop was something like 6♦7♣2♥. This is a somewhat better flop for your cards than 4♦5♣9♥ with your same tens. You do pick up another three outs on the turn (to your opponents' two-pair) yielding an eight-out hand (4.75-to-1).

When three flush cards have flopped and you believe that an opponent has made a flush, if you hold the Ace or King (or first or second highest ranking not on the board) of that suit you can often draw. You no longer have nine outs, though, you only have seven outs (2.59-to-1). When you hold the King (or second highest ranking flush card) you must adjust upwards in your requirements for the size of the pot to account for those times when you lose to the player with the Ace (or highest ranking) in the same suit. If you can accurately put one of your opponents on the nut draw, it is best to fold.

These decisions should not be close enough to the quoted odds that you must precisely know to the dollar how much money is in the pot. You should be able to keep close track by counting the number of bets that there are in the pot as the hand progresses. If the calls are marginal in these situations, you are not costing yourself anything by throwing away the hand. It is essential to adjust upward as recommended so that you don't mistakenly take a draw that appears profitable, but isn't.

Made Hand — Slow-Play?

When you make your hand on the turn, that is, you hit your flush, straight, or better draw, when is it correct to slow-play? The answer to this question in a $2-$5 spread game is simple. Virtually never. The sophistication level of most of your weak opponents at this level is such that you generally only <u>cost</u> yourself money when you slow-play. Your more skillful opponents won't fall for your traps too often.

Let's take a look at how this works in practice and in theory. This example is a poor slow-play on the flop. One unlucky guy to my right had literally been playing for about three hours, and had seen only five or six flops and had won only one pot. Although he was a selective and skillful player, his patience was running understandably thin. He entered a pot from middle position and there were two other players that saw the flop

The player under the gun bet $5 and the man to my right called, the third player folded. As a player not involved in the pot, and knowing the level of play that the player to my right practiced, I knew his hand to be J-10. I felt that it was a serious mistake to slow-play on his part because the other player in the hand would likely take pause with his call, and then not provide any additional action. Because there was only $6 in the pot after the flop, even if the man to my right held a Q♣8♣ he would have a questionable call, and his hand would be a candidate for a raise. He could not have flopped an open-ended straight-draw — thus my conclusion as to his holding. The only other cards he might have held would be a King with a weak kicker (like K♥10♣), but that would have given him top pair and a straight-draw, and would have again justified a raise. A hand he might have called with was something like (K♥6♥), a hand that I hadn't ever seen him play. The *manner* in which he called led me to believe that he had the straight.

The turn brought a J♦, so the board was K♣Q♥9♠J♦. The first player checked and the second player bet, with the first player just calling. The river was a 10, and the first player bet. The second player called in disgust, and the first player rolled over A♦Q♣ for the nut straight. Had the second player raised on the flop, the first player may have folded. If the first player had called a raise, his mistake would have been huge even if he did catch two perfect cards. Granted, the argument could be made that the second player wasn't going to make any money if he raised and ended the hand, but by smooth calling he reduced the money he could make if the bettor held two-pair. How could he decide that the third player involved (yet to act) would have a reason to call $5, but not $10, and that the original bettor would not call an additional $5? Why would he want them in the pot? The $9 he would profit had he raised is well above the expected average win for J-10 off-suit.

I don't know if it is a trait of human character to try to trap other players when a person gets a strong hand, but most people do slow-play too frequently and without due consideration to the specific situation. When I see a player slow-play a flush when I hold a 'set', even though he ends up winning, I know that he has cost himself money. He will be sorely disappointed when the board pairs and his flush is worthless.

When you find yourself against someone whose call is more dangerous than most players' raises, go ahead and draw to beat the best possible hand. That is, if the best possible hand he can have is a straight, draw for a bigger straight, a flush, or better. This advice might seem obvious, but on countless occasions I have seen players draw to a losing hand, when another player (slow-player) already has a hand that they won't beat with their draw.

How does this work in theory? Let's take an example from a game where five players enter the pot for one $2 bet. Let's say that you are in middle position with a hand like

Now the flop comes

My point in this section is not how you play the flop, but rather what happens afterward. For instance, you might check-raise on a semi-bluff, bet or check and call depending on how you would best gain money from the other players. Let's say that you have checked and called with two other callers. The pot size is now $23 (don't forget the rake!). The turn card is the 8♣. So the board is

Are you tempted to slow-play? To address this dilemma, let's take a look at the finances. We know that most players with the A♣ will call with or without correct pot odds, but what about that player in the seat to your left with K♥J♣?

What if you check and it's checked all around? There are seven clubs unseen and 44 unseen cards (your opponent assumes you have the flush made) giving 5.3-to-1 odds for him to out draw you. If there is no bet, you have charged him $0 to win at least $32 (assuming you call on the river). These are not the kind of odds a poker player wants to lay! It becomes obvious that you cannot let your opponents see the next card for free. Ideally, you would like to charge as much as possible for your opponents to see the next card, unfortunately you are in a limit poker game and it is difficult to charge enough to make it incorrect for your opponents to call.

If you bet, and no one but the player with K♥J♣ calls, the pot would be offering that single player 5.4-to-1 on a 5.3-to-1 bet. You are betting in a situation where if there wasn't any money in the pot, your opponent would only be able to call correctly for $0.83! Most poker players would gladly bet $1,000 or more if they were true 5-to-1 favorites, and this is exactly what you should do (for $5) when you bet with the best hand even though it can be out drawn by another hand.

Let's compare this to the situation where you are against a player with K♥J♣ who would allow you to slow-play the hand to the maximum. Your intentions would be to check and call, then check-raise on the river. What if you got an additional caller on the turn who had slow-played 3♦3♠? After the turn, there would be $37 in the pot (one bet and call from three players). Let's review the cards that make each player a winner. Any 3, K, 8 or 6 (nine cards) give the player with the 3's a winner. Any club, other than the 6♣, (six cards) give the player with the K♥J♣ a winner. The remaining cards (27 cards) keep your hand the best. Of course, you are not privy to the exact details of this situation, but the odds won't be much different from this if you've read the hands somewhat accurately. The player with the K♥J♣ is 6-to-1 on a 6.4-to-1 pot, a close call, but one most players in this game will still make. The person with the 'set' is 3.7-to-1 to make his hand, and you are a 1.85-to-1 **favorite to win.** If both players, or even one of the two players, realize that you have a flush, they may not bet on the river at all, (in case you check-raise), and you will have made an expensive mistake. This example may be somewhat out of the ordinary, as both hands still have a chance to beat you.

Consider what would happen if there was a fire in the casino as the fourth card hit the board. You would be unable to complete the hand. On the surface, it appears as if the 3's would get 21% of the pot, your hand would pay 65%, and the K-J would pay 14%. In reality, we must take into account the actual play of the hands on the river as it would likely occur and adjust accordingly. The 3's don't have to pay off a bet if a 4th club falls, and the K♥J♣ probably won't bet hoping just to win in a showdown. Your hand may be paid off by both hands if a blank falls, and if the 3's fill up, you and the K♥J♣ will probably both pay off a bet. You can see that the K♥J♣'s position is even worse than it seems.

Often, one (or more) of your opponents will be drawing dead. The more skillful your opponents the less likely they will fall for your trap, and you lose money by trying to spring it on weak players! So don't slow-play unless you are specifically trying to entice a bluff or throw a new wrinkle in your play to create an impression that you can exploit for more money later.

Baye's Theorem

Baye's Theorem can be helpful to determine your opponent's hand if you know the way he will play a variety of hands. It even applies to opponents you don't know well, but can stereotype. The theorem uses relative probabilities to determine the probability of a specific event. Its utility is best illustrated by an example: A player raises and you know that this player will raise before the flop **only** with Aces, Kings, Queens, and Ace-King suited. You hold A♦Q♦. What is his most likely hand? If you guessed Kings, you already have an intuitive feel for Baye's Theorem. Let's see why. The hands he could hold are:

{A♣A♥, A♣A♠, A♥A♠},{Q♣Q♥, Q♣Q♠, Q♥Q♠},{K♣K♦, K♣K♥, K♣K♠, K♦K♥, K♦K♠, K♥K♠}, or {A♣K♣, A♥K♥, A♠K♠}. Of these possible hands, your opponent will hold Kings 40% of the time and each of the other hands 20% of the time.

Let's look at a more complicated method of using this tool. Take an opponent who'll raise with hands as weak as Q♣10♦, A♦5♦, or 4♣4♥. We'll define him to raise 230 out of 1326 hands. You hold 9♥9♠. Your Nines will be a big favorite to win in a showdown against 13% (smaller pairs), a big underdog to 13% (bigger pairs) and a small to medium favorite to the remaining 74%. Given this information, you would like to play for more money (raise). You are usually going to look at a flop that contains one or more over-cards. This is where Baye's theorem comes in handy. Take the times that you have established through pre-flop play that you aren't against a bigger pair. If a Jack flops, what are the relative chances that he holds a Jack? There are 48 of these hands (Q-J, K-J, and A-J), while 150 won't contain a Jack. In this specific example you are ~ 3-to-1 to be safe with the flop! You can frequently bet or raise as if he missed.[1] On your own, you can determine that the chances of his holding an Ace are closer to 2-to-1 against.

---

1.   This is based on a very predictable player to illustrate the application of Baye's Theorem. Read Sklansky's <u>Getting The Best Of It</u> for a more complete explanation of this great tool.

RIVER PLAY

The Never Ending Struggle To Save Bets

An extremely challenging facet of your play will be trying to save bets at the end of a hand. All five cards will be exposed, and you will have to make a quick decision as to the chances of your hand being the best, as you wager an extra bet for the entire pot. **I can't over emphasize how important this decision is.** You can't always call on the end, because it will be difficult to make up for all the $5 bets you've put into the pots. You must also be judicious folding hands that could be winners, because any mistake will cost you numerous bets. You are bound to make errors in either case, but you want to try to make as few of these misjudgments as possible.

You will improve in this regard as your experience increases, and in particular when you become more skillful at reading your opponents. Straight-forward opponents allow you to fold in more situations than do your tricky adversaries, but even players that **seem** not to be larcenous, often are.

So what is the best approach in the typical $2-$5 game? If the pot is large (greater than 12 bets) you will fare better if you seldom fold with a hand that has a reasonable chance to win the pot. Usually, when you clearly have no chance to win (e.g., when there are four of a suit on board and there are five callers) you should fold. Against only one opponent, that may or may not have the best hand — not to mention a bluffing hand — it is frequently correct to call (sometimes raising is better).

What I try to establish in my mind is the likelihood that my hand is the best, adjusted for the chance that my opponent has something other than what he's representing. If the pot is large enough, I call. If I'm in a pot against several opponents, I gauge each caller by what **he** would think might be the best hand. I over-call (or perhaps raise) only if my chances are: Favorable for having the best hand when compared to the size of the pot, or that stronger hands will fold, leaving me with the best hand.

It would be conjecture on your part to come up with any percentage figures that could be used accurately. These general considerations are what you need to contemplate: For those of you who like assigning probabilities to uncertain events, then do it that way. For others, who prefer to 'get a feel' for whether the situation is favorable or not, that's okay too (if you are skillful in this area). It is the **thought process** that you must go through each and every time you are involved in a hand to the river, and even then you may be unsure as to the status of your hand. Often, an erroneous call is a smaller mistake than a bad fold.

Sometimes you must call a bet that you would not ordinarily pay off. This happens when your opponent *might* bet into a board that **indicates** that he has what you're representing beat. He plays the power of a threatening board, into a better hand, but believes that your hand is not strong enough for **you** to call. I am talking about a player who is playing you **specifically**. Again, try to figure out if he would do this more frequently than the money in the pot will reward your payoff of one $5 bet and either fold or call depending on your conclusion.

Betting For Value

An area in expert play that even some otherwise skillful players don't take advantage of, is betting for value. This is a part of your poker game that may make the difference in several bets over a single session, and will affect your win-rate greatly in a month's time. Betting for value is a term that means: Betting with what should figure to be the best hand into a player that will call you with many hands, some of which might be better than yours. I am not going to cover the theory entirely, but there is excellent work already available on this topic (Read Sklansky's Theory of Poker, Malmuth's Gambling Theory and Other Topics, Norman Zadeh's Winning Poker Systems, and Ciaffone's Improve Your Poker).

If you take a moment to think about this subject, you will realize that the players you are facing in a hand greatly determine the frequency with which you should make a bet with what may or may not be the best hand. What I'm specifically trying to address in this section, is players who are passive and will call with any variety of hands, but who won't call without a pair.

You are faced with a different situation in a typical $2-$5 game than you would be in a tougher game, in that there may be players in the game who have no idea what they're doing. While this is good, it can present you with challenges in regard to your correct betting frequency on the river with a legitimate hand. Ordinarily, you determine your betting action on the river by the types of hands that your opponent will:

1) Call, but not Raise.
2) Bet, but not Call.
3) Bet, but not Call a Raise.
4) Neither Call nor Bet.

In a $2-$5 game, these considerations still apply for all your opponents, but frequently the only concept that matters is #1. Your opponent may **just** call with a variety of hands from those which are weak (bottom pair) to those which are fairly strong (a small flush).

If you have no way to categorize your opponent's calling hand, then you must bet on the basis of the strength of your own hand and what your opponent might think of **his own hand**. That is, you must bet expecting him to call you more often with a losing hand than with a winning hand. This seems obvious, but in practice it is more difficult than it sounds.

Every time you don't bet on the end with the best hand when your opponent would call, you cost yourself a bet, and every time you are called on the end when you have the second best hand, you cost yourself a bet. This appears to be an even money proposition, but it isn't. You still must show a profit even accounting for the times that your opponent makes an extremely strong hand and raises. Against a very weak, 'Calling Station', you won't have to call the additional bet, but against more aggressive players, you have to pay some bets off (you value bet less frequently into this type of opponent). You **should** bet when there are many possible hands that your opponents will call with that you can beat. In most cases, plan on your opponents calling. Bet when you will *usually* be happy that they called. If you never bet losing hands, you're not betting for value enough. Some additional tips that should prove useful:

- If you have top-pair with a medium-kicker and a three-straight (or flush) is on board, bet less frequently. From an early position this hand is often more profitable picking off bluffs.

- The order a possible flush or straight appeared isn't as important against a **weak** player. He doesn't often think about your probable hand, but just the best possible hand. With a scary board, don't bet marginal hands into a weak opponent. They *almost never* fold winners. Save this move for good players.

If the board is *non-threatening*, you'll be surprised how often you can bet a mediocre hand against a weak player (or habitual bluffer), and get called with an inferior hand. Take their money.

Checking To Encourage Bets

Because your game will have a correct mix of betting with made hands (where you have what your are representing), as well as drawing hands, your opponents will often be guessing where you actually are in a hand. Good. Your posture will usually be one of aggressive action, and this will often lead your opponents into making errors betting against you if you indeed have changed pace. In other words, when you check on fourth street, you may not necessarily be weak or on a draw, but many of your opponents will read you this way. This will create an urge for them to bet their weaker hands, and you can often pick up bets when otherwise they might not have called your bet.

This arises when you are not certain that you have the best hand. You need a hand that will beat many of your opponent's hands which he would fold if you bet again, and where free cards aren't a problem if you are beat. For instance, you hold

And the flop comes

When you bet on the flop and are just called by a fairly aggressive player, you may already have the second best hand. A player might call a bet with a J-10, or similar (like Q-10), so he may have a (weak) draw. Other players will just call with an Ace that

may have a weaker kicker than your 7♦. At the same time, you could easily be out-kicked by this player. Usually, only if a 7 or a diamond falls on the turn would you go ahead and bet again. If on the turn, your opponent — first to act — checks, go ahead and check behind him. He may bet a weaker hand on the river trying to pick up the pot. If you are first to act you can either check and fold, or pay off his bets to the river (depending on your opponent).

Another time this situation arises is when you have flopped a four flush with a pair. You hold

and the flop comes

You will usually want to bet this hand on the flop, but on the turn, if you fear that you have an inferior hand (the flush doesn't come and someone might have an ace), you may want to check (depending on the action and number of players in the pot). A suspicious opponent may put you solely on a flush-draw, and if the third card to the flush doesn't come on the river, he may bet into you trying to bluff. Notice, you will have to make a judgment call as to the strength of your pair compared to the cards that fall on the turn and river, but you will be surprised how often you will have the best hand in this situation.

Worried About Being Check-Raised?

One challenge that you will run into by being an aggressive player is that you will get check-raised fairly frequently. Your stronger playing opponents will need to hinder your aggression so that they don't get run over with all the other timid players. This will usually take place on the flop or the turn. Suck-out-players will also gleefully check-raise you when they've made some unlikely catch.

You will still want to bet for value with many of your hands on the river, even those as weak as top pair with a strong kicker. Be prepared to see that unpleasant extra stack of chips flying in the pot when someone has made their hand. This usually occurs when you are in a late position and your opponents know you will bet, (because you frequently do). A check-raise on the river must be treated somewhat differently than on the other streets, because it almost always comes from a hand that the raiser doesn't think you can beat. It may be from a horrendous three-out draw to a weak kicker or a gut-shot that makes it. Unless you have a stronger hand than your opponent thinks you have (get inside their head for a second), lay down your hand. This is almost never a bluff, even if the player is an absolute lunatic, or an expert.

Of course, don't bet yourself into obvious check-raising situations. If your opponent was drawing to a straight or a flush don't fall into the weak trap by betting for him. You can't fear every possible straight or flush that appears either. Try to put your opponent on a hand, and then bet as if you *know* what his two cards are. If you're wrong and chips start flying, then just fold.

GENERAL
ADVICE

Avoiding Common Errors

In day to day play at the tables in the $2-$5 games, there are often fairly decent players who suffer some minor weaknesses in their games. Any one of which might make the difference between a break-even player and a winner, but when added up a losing player emerges.

Along the path toward proficient play, there are some immediate steps that a player can take to affect substantially his expectation. Simply put, it is to stop making minor errors that cost money. The following sections are written to help you accomplish this goal in the shortest time possible.

To give you an example to which type of error I'm referring, I'll point out a habit in play that a tight player (and quite friendly guy) made in a game recently. Whenever this man was in a pot with anyone heads up, he would announce "Just you and me? Then I check." This person was always in these situations with the best hand, if not the nuts. He allowed free cards in this manner six times over the period of about seven hours.

He even did it to me once, and I'd just met him! I flopped two-pair when three hearts flopped. I came out betting and he just called. I was extremely concerned with the possibility that he had flopped a flush, so I was happy to pull off two free cards. I had a chance to make a full house, when I might not have even called if he had raised. Anyway, he said, "Just you and me? Then I check." Well, I certainly was going to **take** the free cards. He held the A♥Q♥!

Over the period of the evening, I calculated this habit to cost him at least $70. This is $10 per hour! It was no surprise to me that he mentioned in passing that he had been running badly. Hopefully, the following writings will keep you from making this type of error.

Common Error #1
Not Staying Emotionally Detached

It is important not to get emotionally involved with your game, with another player, or with any one hand. This can often be the demise of an otherwise solid player. In fact, it is one reason I recommend extensive play on computers. While it is true that computers haven't attained the upper levels of skill necessary to beat an expert, (at least those I've played) they do have some excellent training uses.

First of all, when you play against a computer, you see so many hands, that *nothing* surprises you when it happens. You can literally play a computer game at the rate of 100 to 200 hands per hour. This represents up to five hours of simulated play per hour of computer time. The computers also do have some skills! I believe that based on pure card playing decisions, a computer would win money in weaker games. The problem is that a computer won't learn enough from the previous play of opponents. It also won't keep track of hands that its opponent likely holds when the board develops into something scary. For instance, if there is substantial pre-flop raising by a tight opponent — then the board ends up being 4♣5♥6♦7♣2♥ — the computer might fold even if it had aces! I do believe that these weaknesses will be overcome eventually.

The true strength of the computer is to show how the techniques of semi-bluffing, keeping track of pot odds, and figuring player types for down cards can and do work. Meanwhile it builds a detached level of confidence in you, and you learn that the game can be beaten and that *you* can beat it.

I think of poker as a war over which I'm the General. The cards are my troops and the chips are my artillery. I always want to have enough troops to make my artillery barrages worthwhile and I always want to have enough artillery to support my troops. Heaven forbid that I have some Ace troops stranded without any mortars or guns to beat my enemy into submission. Yes, sometimes it's true, the enemy has enough troops and ammunition to cost you a battle. If you have enough artillery, though, you'll be able to raise more troops. In other words, bring enough money to allow yourself to maximize your profits on your good hands, yet be mentally prepared to suffer some casualties.

I can't emphasize enough how hard you should work to keep your emotions in control. You think more clearly when you are not angry, and you are less likely to play your hand in a pot in which you don't belong. Discipline is the key to success in this area. It's hard to stay calm when a player has caught a two-card 'out' for the third time in a session, but it's absolutely essential for your success.

There will be times when you will be astounded by the number of bad beats that players put on you. It will seem as if they cannot miss their two and three card outs. These are the times that will test your sanity. You can have more bad sessions than seems possible and your opponents can catch two perfect cards with a fantastic frequency. Try not to let it get you down. It is difficult during a streak like this to keep your self-esteem. You may wonder if you really know how to play the game at all. Don't stray from your course. Your bad run **will** pass with time. They can't continue to draw out on you. Continue to evaluate your own game and confirm that you are playing well in *good* games and you will win. Your longevity is assured while they will likely be looking to a different source of income for their next buy-in.

Common Error #2
Mercy Doesn't Apply To Poker Chips

How many times have you been playing in a game, and the pot comes down to two players who know each other? One of the players will say, "Oh, it's just you and me?", they'll roll over their cards and play showdown or something similar. The idea being that, 'all these other players are strangers enough for me to take their money, but since we're buddies, we won't get into any confrontations.' This idea is ridiculous. It's analogous to refusing to take your opponent's queen in chess when you've trapped her. It's against the nature of the game. If you aced your opponent in tennis, you certainly wouldn't say, "Oh, let me hit a serve that you can return."

This type of behavior tends to breed some animosity in other players, and the soft play really is silly. The other side of the argument is that other players are happy to get on to another hand, (when they aren't involved in a pot). I don't know about you, but I usually become friendly with many of my opponents, but I don't give any quarter, and don't expect any in return. It's often *more* confusing when a friendly opponent changes his play when you're in a hand, than when he just plays his ordinary game.

This brings up a related subject of Team Play. Personally, I don't think that much team play occurs at a limit this small. While I'm sure that there could be a winning team play, it is illegal and I think that a player would be *much* better off learning to play at an expert level on an individual basis.

My thinking is, if two players are playing together in Hold'em, what advantage would they have over me?   Well, they might signal the value or specific makeup of each other's hand, and they could try to raise me continually as one teammate takes the worst of it. The other in agreement, would later share the win. Would this be worth it? Basically, it would have the effect of decreasing the payoff I would be receiving for some of my drawing hands, but they still wouldn't know what my hand is!   If I have the ability to put at least one of them on a hand — and it really doesn't matter which one — I'll be able to determine the value of my hand with any corresponding draws. So, unless the players were good players, as well as expert teammates, I believe my game wouldn't suffer too much. But it would suffer enough. I would discourage play in games where *suspected* partnerships are operating and support a "square" game. In addition, I would report the suspected activity to the poker room manager.

I've also seen mercy extended to weak or to new players. I think that there can be reasons to support this type of ploy with the idea that mercy is really not merciful. You will often come across a player that is so bad, that he will be putting money into the game at a rate ensuring his rapid poverty. He may enjoy the game, but he usually will find a game where his money lasts longer. Sometimes a bit of soft-play can keep the person interested enough to come back and play with the "fun folks" that occupy your table. This might occur when you know you've got him beat dead to rights, and you announce your hand, or roll over your cards as you place your last bet. Remember, the money he has would be useful to the poker economy, and some encouragement to "keep trying" will sometimes make lifetime players out of these folks. The other argument is that a player like this is going to lose his money so fast that you better take your share while he has some left! This is a judgment call.

Common Error #3
The Decision To Show Down Your Hand

Many players have strange idiosyncrasies when it comes to the act of showing down their poker hands after all the cards are on the board. Some players will take their cards in one hand, stare at them and rub them in disgust before mucking them. Others will wait with mediocre hands or what might be considered embarrassing, two-card holdings, until they're sure that they have the best hand, and then roll it over. This is a form of slow rolling. It usually occurs because the player is somewhat ashamed of his play.

Why would these methods be a disadvantage? Rarely will you see solid, winning players exhibit these tendencies for several reasons:

- Most winning players want to play as many hands per hour as possible to increase their expected hourly gain.

- Their starting hands are usually respectable enough to withstand any scrutiny, and they *know* the reason they played the way they did.

- Any winning hand is worth showing, and doesn't require any explanation or excuse.

- When you turn your hand face up you have a built in "quality check", as the dealer can verify the winning hand.

- You *appear* confident when you are sure of your holdings, and people will appreciate your poker etiquette.

- Players frequently display disgusted looks when they're losing and they make attractive targets.

It always amazes me when someone shows great disgust at

missing a flush-draw or straight-draw. These draws only come in about one third of the time, and *nobody* will feel sympathy if another player misses. It is a behavior almost exclusively associated with the losers of the game that believe in "good luck" and "bad luck", not those that understand the mathematics of the game.

You will make fewer errors by just rolling over your cards when you think you have a shot at the pot. However, it is also in your best interest to conceal some of your playing habits from your more clever opponents. When you have missed one of your draws, you can muck your hand as soon as you see a hand that beats yours. Keep in mind, that in this game you will be using your sophisticated plays rarely against certain players, and the rest of the time you will be playing pretty straight forward, quality cards. In other words, you will be calling with your draws and betting your hands. It often works out, then, that you would be more inclined to show down a draw that you had semi-bluffed with sometime during the hand, *if players were always folding when you bet.* Try to control the frequency with which your opponents call by choosing the hands you show down to influence their ideas on how you are playing. If nobody ever calls you, perhaps show them a four flush that you bet on a semi-bluff. If everybody calls, only show them strong hands.

Some players are trying to convince their opponents that they are making a tough lay down when they look at their cards and feign breaking them — nobody is fooled. Even the most novice players know that this is a facade and just a waste of time.

Common Error #4
Betting And Raising Goofs

It is my opinion that all bets should be for the maximum amount, and all raises should be for the maximum amount. With certain exceptions like playing short-handed (i.e., you risk breaking up the game by annoying *gambling* players or you *want* them to make mistakes calling you) always raise or bet the maximum amount. By doing so, you will keep your opponents guessing at the makeup of your hand, and they will have no additional information regarding the *category* or *type* of hand you're playing. The same goes for the turn and the river. In other words, you don't want to divulge information as whether you would like callers, or you would like to take the pot right then. Frankly, when I'm playing in a low-limit game of any kind, I'll win more money per hour if my opponents fold their hands more readily than if I get plenty of action. This *is* the fine balance that you have to try to control. Ideally, you'd be in a game where you get action on your big hands, and total respect on your vulnerable hands. This is a rare phenomenon, and you will at best be trying to *create* a game environment that approaches this utopia.

Try to make your betting motion the same on every bet. Until you get to the point where you feel comfortable enough with your habits to use fake tells, it's better not to pretend to act at all. Just bet your hand, and wait for the action to come to you again. I would recommend not trying to act as if your hand is worthless when you have a "monster", nor acting like you're holding a powerhouse when you're bluffing, until you have planned it as part of a "bigger" strategy. Most decent players will ignore any overt acts and look more into the play of your hand. Let me give you an example:

I was playing in a game with one fairly strong and creative player, and one ordinary player. The pot was un-raised before the flop, and I held A♥9♥ in the blind. The flop came Q♣5♥9♦. I bet, and both players called. I knew the strong player didn't have a Queen because he would have raised, and the other player called with almost anything, so I had no idea what he had. The turn card came 6♦. I bet again and this time the strong player raised! The weak player folded, but I thought, "What can the raise mean?" The 6♦ would have been a gut-shot, and I knew that this player wouldn't have called needing such a card, and he also wouldn't have called with 5-6 or even 9-6 (which he wouldn't even play). I figured that he was semi-bluffing with a draw. By the way, this player wouldn't have slow-played a Q-9 either. I then knew that I had to raise! The river was a 2♣ and I knew I was in good shape. I checked to pick off a bluff (which he didn't make), rolled over my hand, and my opponent mucked his cards.

The point of the story is, not only would acting tactics not accomplish anything, but even a strong raise didn't accomplish anything because my opponent played inconsistently with what he was trying to represent. I believe he had over-cards to the 9 (like maybe K-10). Had he raised on the flop he probably could have made me throw my hand away, but by waiting until the turn came, I was sure the turn didn't make his hand better than mine. This is based on how I thought that he would consider what cards *I* held. The same goes for amateur acting. It may work against neophytes in the game, but they aren't usually watching what other players are doing. I would spend more time trying to make sure I didn't have any subtle tells that gave away information to the good players.

MINOR STRATEGIC CONSIDERATIONS

Ignoring Other Players' Advice

It seems that no matter at what table you play, sometime in the session you will get someone giving advice on how the game of Texas hold'em should be played. Eventually, this gets more tiresome than bad beat stories because it may be aimed directly at you, and it's accuracy in terms of theory may be totally incorrect.

To give you an example: There is one man who regularly comes into the pot for $5 in the $2-$5 spread-limit game. He does it with such frequency and a with wide variety of hands, that it makes it difficult to put him on any specific hand before the flop. While I don't advocate such play, it does make it necessary for you to adjust the type of hands you will play and how you will play them.

Basically, if you are to his right, you have a tool available to build big pots for hands that play well in multi-way pots (e.g., A♣Q♣). So from a middle position it works well to have him make it $5 after you have called for $2 because you can then re-raise the maximum. However, if you have something like 10♣10♠ or J♦J♠ or maybe even a pair of 9's, it might be necessary to raise to the maximum from your same position. The reason being, if you just call and he makes it $5, (you have the intention to re-raise), what you've done is create a pot in which you need to flop a 'set' to feel comfortable about your hand. Good players and bad alike will chase with the larger pot odds they are getting, and you may have set yourself up for your hand not to win.

If you're sitting to his left, then the theory works in just the reverse. If he comes in for $5, and you have a hand that plays well in a short-handed pot, it is mandatory to re-raise even if it means you play heads-up with your A♦A♠ to his 8♠7♠. You won't win much money, but it is worth it to take the large advantage of the small pots rather than give the whole table a chance to out-draw you.

What will happen as this person comes in time and time again for $5 is that other players will not respect his raise at all. If you **just** call with hands that are as weak as A♦10♣, you will often get yourself into a pot where your chances of winning are poor. So, think about folding M∅ hands, and raising with S∅ hands.

My method for dealing with this player on one occasion (he was sitting to my immediate right) was to call his $5 bet with hands that required larger implied odds (like medium-small pairs and medium suited connectors — S∞ and M∞). I re-raised to $10 with a strong hand that plays well short-handed, (like A♦J♥ or K♣Q♥ — M♥, M∅, and S♣). I folded most other hands. (If other players start routinely calling your re-raise then you must change your strategy.)

My goal was to make his poker life miserable and to interfere with his method of play. After I had made this play a few times, the man to my right again raised to his standard $5. I re-raised with K♦K♠. He immediately, (with hostility) said, "Why do you always want to get it heads-up, why don't you build a pot!?" I told him, politely, "That is the way **you** play; that is **not** the way I play." He folded when I bet on the flop, and stormed off in a huff to play in a different game. While I think it is amusing that he felt this way, my real point is: Don't let other players dictate how you should play the game so they can manipulate the pot the way they want. Rather, do what is necessary to create the size and number of players in a pot that **you** desire.

Another example of ignoring advice (perhaps unwisely) came in an evening when I was sitting just to the right of an extremely tight player. His play was quite solid and the hands he rolled over were high quality. I thought his play was probably too tight for the game we were in, but he seemed to be winning and I presumed that he was (and is) a consistent winner. The interesting part of the story is that he was friendly toward me and was fairly open to advising me on how to play. Most of his input was fairly general. Once he said, "You seem to be getting into pots with pretty good hands, but some times you are just a bit too aggressive." — Which is possibly true. On one particular hand, though, I had K♣K♠, raised and had one caller. A different player to my right was complaining for some reason about my raise even though he wasn't in the hand. I had become greatly distracted by the player doing the lobbying, when my opponent bet as the final card appeared, placing three diamonds on the board, which I didn't notice. I quickly raised (foolishly), and my opponent only called, rolling over K♦3♦ for the flush. My advisor said, "You know, you've already got the money in the pot, why do you need to push it?" It was a very poor raise, but I think he missed the reason for my stupid play, which was the loud objector to my right.

The amusing part of this story is that this experienced player flashed his hole cards **every** hand. It was so blatant that I couldn't avoid seeing them without even looking away from my own hand. This gave me quite a bit of insight into his playing standards. I didn't feel good about taking advantage of this knowledge (unless I could bust him with it). I thought that since his intent to help me to become a better player was genuine, I would help him. I mentioned the fact that he was accidentally exposing his cards, and he humbly thanked me.

Who knows how much our own bad habits cost us at the table? When a solid player offers advice, it's worth considering. When a donating player offers advice, it's worth trying to make money using it against him.

Playing Versus "All-in" Players

For some strange reason, there are many players at the tables who seem to enjoy playing with few chips in front of them. I don't know if they prefer to score a big win off a small buy-in or perhaps they just enjoy seeing all five board cards as cheaply and as frequently as possible. Many of these players have plenty of money to play the game, but for their own reasons, they always buy in for the minimum $20. I do not believe this is a good strategy. These same players often complain when they finally are dealt the 'nuts' and then run out of money! I have, at times put an excess of $100 on a single hand with the 'nuts', and always want the flexibility to do so. Since I won't be taking draws that are not worthwhile (if I can help it), I want to be able to capitalize on any hand that ends up being the best. You can't do this if you run out of chips! My experience tells me that successful poker players are supplied with ample chips on the table.

Even though a "few chips" strategy may not be sound, you still will be confronted with some challenges when playing against one of these players. First, you must always be aware of how much money he has in front of him. If you try a bluff or a semi-bluff when he is just about out of chips, you're in trouble because he will go "all-in". In addition, if he has no more chips, you won't be getting any implied odds from him on draws that materialize. You must make your decision to take the draw on the merits of the pot size as it stands (heads-up).

If you are in a multi-way pot, and one or more players go "all-in", you must decide what strategy is the most effective for your hand. I've seen many players stop most betting action (other than calling) when they are fearful that the "all-in" player has the best hand. This is incorrect. If you are going to bother calling, you either want other players or you don't. To give an example: Say you had top pair and a good kicker, but you were concerned that the "all-in" player had a 'set' (maybe he went "all-in" for $2). If you are going to consider calling, you need to decide whether it is profitable to try to collect money from the rest of the players in the hand. Notice that if you raise, you may well isolate the hand to you and the "all-in" player. This would not be prudent if you knew he had you badly beaten, you might as well fold. If there is a chance you have him beaten or he's not that far ahead (perhaps he has two small pair), then raising would be an excellent strategy (just like other times when you may have the second best hand). Your raise doesn't cost you anything if no one else calls, but it may accomplish exactly the same thing as a raise that cost $5. If someone calls with a third best hand you have still made a good raise. You certainly **wouldn't** want to raise (on a semi-bluff) while drawing to a hand that may beat everyone that still has money, but lose to the "all-in" player.

Another habit that many of these "all-in" players have, is raising to $7 with a marginal hand when they are down to their last $9 or $10. They fully have the intention of going "all-in" on the next card. After watching these players for some time, you may get a feel for the type of hands with which they will make this play. If they only do it with strong hands, then don't give them action. If they do it with strange hands, re-raise with your good ♥, ♦ and ♣ hands and make them play their "cheese" against your quality hands. Never stop busting these players. They **can** interfere with your style of play, and you don't need to feel sorry for them.

Playing 11 Handed

Occasionally, the poker rooms you play in will squeeze an additional player into a normal table to make the game consist of eleven players. While the general playing theory remains consistent, you will be getting a different makeup in the number of players taking flops, and this requires some changes in your strategy.

What tends to happen is that the players in late positions will see more players enter the pot before them, and will use this as an excuse to come into the pot. They justify this more liberal play because of the increased pot odds, but that is not entirely correct. Remember, each player only adds $2 to the pot, but his mere presence gives much better implied odds when you flop a good hand.

The changes in strategy required are mainly focused around eliminating opponents when you have a vulnerable hand, and to increase your payoff on your drawing hands by making the pot larger when facing many opponents. Previously, I mentioned that the need to check-raise is diminished in this $2-$5 limit. The risk of no one betting and thus allowing a free card often outweighs the penalty you pay by not eliminating some of the competition when you bet right out. An opponent is making more costly errors when he calls your $5 bet, than he does in a fixed-limit game. However, when that single extra player enters the game, you will be in situations where you must risk a free card to limit the field. An example would be when you hold a hand like Q♣10♥ in the blind, and the flop comes Q♥5♦7♦. A check is in order, and indeed, if many players enter the pot for a single bet before the action gets back to you, you're often better off folding. If a bet comes from a late position player you should often raise. Even here you might consider folding depending on the player that puts in the bet and whether any players call in between the two of you. Be more inclined to raise, if the player bets on semi-bluffs or with hands like A♣7♣. Tend toward folding if this player usually bets only top pair or better.

If you flop a draw in early position, you can often call a single bet that comes immediately from your right. Enough players will come into the pot behind you that you will be getting a good return on your draw. This might happen if you hold 7♠8♠ and the flop comes K♣5♥6♥. Notice that because of the two hearts, you might not take this draw in a 10 handed game with few players in the pot. When there are seven or eight players taking a look at the flop, your payoff is generally better. It might be argued that because of the larger number of hands you're facing, the chances of a player holding a flush-draw is increased, and therefore you should be **less** likely to take this draw. Your concern should be the payoff you get from the other players in the hand. There are still six cards that will give you your straight and that won't make someone else a flush. The other thing that becomes important, is that although a player might play any two suited cards, he can never be confident of his hand when his cheesy flush develops. He sometimes won't even bet the flush when it hits because it is so weak.

With your big wired pairs you have an increased challenge. You like to get more money in the pot, and you want to limit the competition; therefore, you should be inclined to raise. Sometimes this will not accomplish the latter goal, (especially if you are in early position and the player to your immediate left calls). If you can avoid falling in love with your hand, and release it when it becomes clear that you are beaten — beyond a reasonable return from the pot to draw to your hand — you will be playing profitably. In early position, with very vulnerable pairs like Jacks and Tens, if you can eliminate players with your raises, do so. Otherwise you may prefer to call, (and see if you like the flop), or re-raise a late position raiser. If this still doesn't eliminate the competition, you better hope you flop a 'set' because it's sometimes correct to take long shot draws in these pots, and everyone will.

Have a heyday with the ∞ and ☯ type hands. There is almost no way to misplay the stronger of these types before the flop, and the weaker ones can work to manipulate your competitors' perception of you. For instance, if you are getting players that think they can ignore your presence when small cards flop, you can occasionally raise in an early position with a hand like 9♣7♣. This will give them something to ponder if you get to show the hand. This will not usually be necessary in a typical game.

Sometimes it is to your benefit that some of your opponents really do **know** what you have. You want some of your astute opponents to fold hands like middle pair with an over-card kicker. For example, you may hold K♣Q♦ in an early-middle position. If the flop comes K♠8♥2♣, it is in your interest to have a hand like A♦8♦ fold. A good player will consider either raising or folding this hand (when the pot is not large enough to justify a call). In these eleven-handed games, he knows that he will not always accomplish the goal of knocking out other players (hands like K♥4♥) with a raise, so he is better off folding. He can do this with a clear conscience because he knows that you have **at least** top pair. You can sometimes get away with betting a pair of 9's in the same way, but be hesitant to bet a wired pair lower than 8's unless you are against only a few prudent players. Certainly, if anyone calls, you are finished with the hand unless you improve considerably.

Playing Short-handed

It is inevitable that you will be presented with the option of playing in a short-handed game (six players or less). Many players choose to avoid these situations for several reasons. One is that the rake can become too costly for the stakes that are involved. Another thing that weak players don't like is that the hands are often contested heads-up for small pots. Generally, the game can become dull if there is not at least one aggressive player and others willing to play faster than normal. If you are betting and raising aggressively, your cost per hand will be large in comparison to the money that you can expect to win from a typical opponent, so make sure that you *own* them.

There is *not* great value in stealing blinds ($2) short-handed because they're small in relation to the bets, but you still must attack them. Occasionally raise to $5 or $6 to "sell" your opponent into taking the worst of it. You want your opponent to put more money in the pot when you have a pre-flop advantage. If they often defend for $7 with weak hands then always make them pay. Otherwise, vary your play. The values of hands change in a short-handed game. Big cards become the preferred hands. Don't play weaker drawing hands (M∞ or worse) except for a rare deception. MØ, WØ, any Ace, and pocket pairs are the hands that can be raised as if they were premium cards. You prefer hands that have a good chance to show down the best hand without improvement because you often don't flop anything and you must frequently continue with the hand. If someone is playing an aggressive fixed-limit style of short-handed play — trying to steal blinds and the money from players that have limped into the pot — you don't want that player to run over your hands or blinds. The game will become a big loser for you if you refuse to play back at an aggressive opponent. Trapping plays are hard to come by because you don't get big hands very often. You will go broke if you wait to trap. If the game turns into something with which you are not comfortable, you probably should look for a different game. You must play *poker and people* short-handed.

Types Of Players And How They Affect Your Play

After you have spent some time at a table, you'll notice that the game will take on a personality of its own. The game should have some players who you consider to be poor and unskilled. They can fall into any of the following categories, and the more hands they play with lousy cards, the better. Weak players who are tight don't cost you much, but they don't make you rich either. Beyond these initial considerations lie the basic types of an individual player's weaknesses. Most players at this level have at least one leak in their game, and it is up to you to exploit these holes most profitably.

In the $2-$5 game, you must still be very cognizant of the mathematics in the game. That is, draw when the pot is offering you correct odds to do so, and play hands that expect to make you money over time. At the same time, each opponent that you face gives you the ability to play the player. You can make plays that are profitable against that person, while these same plays might be losers against another person.

To give an example in theory: You are in a pot that contains $100 with an unfamiliar player the first hand of the day and you miss your draw. You would be inclined to bluff on the end **randomly** once out of 20 times. This is the optimal frequency according to game theory when your opponent's calling frequency is unknown. Game theory is beyond the scope of this book, but I do recommend you study it as it applies to poker. (Read Sklansky's The Theory of Poker & Getting The Best of It)

If you have knowledge regarding the play of your opponent, however, you will be required to change the frequency that you will bluff according to the calling frequency of that player. It turns out that the more likely your opponent is to call, the less frequently you should bluff and vice versa. It's not exactly rocket science, but it's important to remember.

These are the kind of changes that allow you to alter your strategy from a winning one to an optimal one. Believe me, the difference can amount to several dollars an hour.

The following chapters describe ways in which you can tailor your game to the specific table at which you are playing. To me, this is where most players that do attain some skill fail to achieve greater success. Even though at the $2-$5 level hold'em is predominately a game of cards, it is **not** a game of showdown or **just** cards. Unveiling the *strategies of the people* who play the cards is where your money lies. Yes, you must play good cards, too, but while doing so, you must continually make adjustments to your opponents in every hand and every game. Keep in mind that the margins for profit are actually fairly small. You can't let opportunities to make extra money pass you by. Every single chip that an opponent puts into the pot that you try not to take when you *know* that you can is money deducted from your win at the end of the year. Frequent small lapses can add up to a large sum of money. When in doubt, *take the money*! Certainly, don't *let* them have it!

Playing Versus Super Aggressive Players (Not Maniacs)

For some reason, when you play $2-$5, you'll get players who love to play aggressively in your game. When this happens, the players at the table will usually exchange dubious glances, buckle down to try to protect their money, and garner as much of the wild money as possible. There can be a sniffing out period in the initial stages when one of these players sits down at the table. Skillful players use this time to distinguish between someone who is extremely aggressive, and someone who is just a lunatic with his money.

The difference is that a skillful, aggressive player can make all your worst hold'em nightmares come true. A maniac might raise five times on a flush-draw, heads-up when you have top 'set', with only $6 in the pot before the flop. He may or may not know what you have, but this is the way he likes to play. By the time he realizes that you have a strong hand, there might be enough money in the pot for him to make a correct call!

This is one place where a good bankroll comes into play. I will put all of my table money in the pot with top 'set' (with the possible exception of being up against a straight-flush draw), and not blink an eye if I lose. (At least until the tears have stopped). Because at my table, I want to be sovereign, and I think, "I have plenty of money set aside just for occasions like this." If you beat him a few times — believe me — you will tranquilize him. If you don't, hang in there!

If you are on a limited bankroll, or prefer a different approach, you can make a play that will still make decent money, still deflate his sails, and perhaps make him tread more lightly when he's in a hand with you. If the hand develops with you flopping top 'set' as described, you can bet once into your opponent (or raise once if you have position) and then call his subsequent raise. Now, regardless of which card falls next, take the aggressive posture with a bet or raise depending on your position. If the card appears to be a blank, raise twice and then call. If it is a card that may have made your opponent's hand, only raise once. You still have 10 outs. What this does is create substantial deception to your hand, and your aggressive adversary probably won't know what you have, but will guess that you have two-pair. Now, when the river card falls, and you **strongly** feel that you have the best hand, you will most likely gain one or two extra bets if he makes a hand that he figures will beat you.

As a side note, these players are generally better at identifying the rank of your hand (flush, straight, two-pair, etc.) than identifying the cards in your hand, because these players often play any two suited cards or any two cards that can make a straight. Their skills in reading the rank of your hand should not be underestimated.

The other alternative is one that will reduce your fluctuations, but also reduce your expectation. That is, to let your opponent drive the betting, while you call along **once you have reduced the competition** to heads-up or maybe to one additional player. In drawing situations you should almost eliminate your semi-bluffs and other deceptive plays, and grab the big payback you deserve when you make your "nut" hand. This allows you a good return on drawing hands, but should reduce some of the "luck" factor with hands that are vulnerable.

Keep in mind, that you still don't want to give free cards, and if over-cards are a threat, you need to take some steps to protect your hand with a bet or raise. If your opponent raises again, and he has the worst hand, he is accomplishing your job, in part, for you. If he has the best hand with some freakish combination of cards that would be difficult to read (e.g., two-pair with 9♣4♦), then you have saved money.

I believe a player should aspire to compete with these players on their playing field and dominate them. The skill involved in playing against players that are comfortable being in precarious situations takes time to develop. Until you have achieved the ability to dominate the specific opponent (or opponents), you need to take steps that make sure you aren't taking the worst of it. This shouldn't be too difficult in a full game. Just stick to quality starting cards and play a slightly more conservative game. If you find yourself in a short-handed game with a couple of these players, you may want to find a different game until you have more practice. Of course, if you're looking for an adventure, the experience gained from short-handed games can be valuable.

Playing Versus Scared Players

I define a scared player as one who is worried about the best possible hand being made among the other players. A player like this rationalizes his play in two ways. One, is that he just **feels** that some player has the best possible hand. There is no logical explanation for this marvel. For instance, two running clubs come on the turn and river putting three clubs on board, but there is nothing to indicate that his opponent has two clubs. If the scared player has the top 'set', he might check on the river because he's afraid of the flush. The other thought he has is: If a player would have called anyway, with some miscellaneous hand, then he was better off not betting, if his opponent ends up making a winning hand by catching a good last card.

Both of these deductions are extremely costly and just plain incorrect. By the way, you will not find successful players who feel this way. A winning player needs to take advantage of almost all situations where he has even a slight edge. The cavity in a player's concerns is not the focus of this section, but rather it is how to effectively exploit his weaknesses.

What you must consider is that this player will raise much less frequently than other opponents, and will be just calling with hands that are often far superior to your own. One mistake that other players make is that they fail to recognize situations where a scared player will be on a draw to hands such as straights and flushes. He doesn't **always** have a strong hand made. On these occasions you must still avoid giving him free cards. You will also notice that a scared player tends to bluff less often than other players (some don't ever bluff). Too many players fail to throw away mediocre hands against a final bet from him.

Generally, you can treat a call from a player like this the way you would treat a raise from a more aggressive player. You must make special note of the board to determine if it's possible that he is on a draw. You won't often find him taking cards with middle pairs or under pairs. If the board doesn't look as if there is an available draw, be careful. If you don't have the best possible kicker with top pair, or better, you may want to slow down. Remember, just because your opponent doesn't bet after you've checked, doesn't mean you have him beat.

Playing Versus 'Calling Stations'

A 'calling station' is a player who just calls almost exclusively and religiously. They rarely raise. Usually they will only raise with the 'nuts' on the river. They will call on a slow-play if they make the hand before the river. They will also call with hands that are seemingly (to ordinary players) unrelated to the flop. The worst of these players are the 'live ones' that all the other players drool over when they approach the table.

As these players improve, they start calling less with hopeless hands, and even occasionally raise with a hand that needs protection (like top pair). You must be aware of possible improvements that are developing in these players because it will affect your optimal strategy.

Most peoples' incomes do not allow them to be 'calling stations' for long, because the habit is extremely expensive. Often someone, usually an 'okay' player will give free lessons to help that 'caller' improve. If the 'calling station' is smart, he will listen to the less than expert advice that some players offer.

The origin of this calling behavior doesn't indicate any lack of intelligence or fault necessarily, but just inexperience. Most of these players have played in home games where *everyone calls*. His priorities might be more focused on placing his bets in turn, or keeping up with the pace of the game. Others just seem to like to call.

How do you make the most money from a player of this nature? You can bet and raise more freely, but rarely on a bluff or semi-bluff. There are times when you can push a bluff through one of these stations, but they are rare. You are almost always better off just showing down your hand when you miss a draw. I've seen 'calling stations' call on the river with a 6 high which played! Personally, I like to encourage him to play, and to show him genuine enthusiasm when he has a good hand (7's full of deuce's with 7♦2♠), and to compliment him when he catches extremely well. You'll find this easier to do when you're not in the hand with him! I want him to have a good time for his money. He's entitled.

Your general playing strategy is the same in a $2-$5 game as most other games against a player like this. You are likely to see more of this type of player at beginner tables that some $2-$5 games comprise.

You can usually play just a straight forward, uncreative game against a 'calling station' to win the most money. This is one reason it may be difficult for another strong opponent to realize your level of skill. When he sees you playing simple 'good hand' poker, he may not adjust his thinking appropriately when the hand is heads-up between the two of you. You too must keep this in mind when using more advanced playing strategies against a stronger player. He will be slower to give you credit for thinking at a high level; sophisticated plays could backfire.

Playing Versus Sandbaggers

This type of player comprises a rather small percentage of players you'll face, and it may sometimes be attributed to a passing phase. These players have difficulty winning because they rarely get value for their hands. Many players draw out on them, which must be quite frustrating.

This is the player who will just call to the river, and then throw in a raise or check-raise. They come in two varieties. One type just wants to make sure that he has the best hand, and, another type just enjoys putting a beat on another player with a double bet on the end. They think that this is the best way to make money. Neither of these strategies has much merit, as discussed earlier, it is rarely correct to slow-play in the $2-$5 game. However, these players do present some challenges to both your mental and financial games.

The easier of the players that you will face is the player that simply calls with big hands with which other players would raise. For instance, if he flops a 'set', two-pair, or even top pair with a huge kicker, he will just call all bets and raises, but won't instigate the action. Sometimes he will even slow-play the hand on the flop. Even in a fixed-limit game (where a player might intend to check-raise on the turn with a double bet) this is rarely a correct strategy. In the $2-$5 game, though, you have gained nothing by waiting, and you have risked a substantial amount by giving a free card.

It is important to distinguish between occasions where he may have a legitimate draw, and those times when you are betting an inferior hand. If there is not a likely draw, you may want to give free cards because you are probably behind. Of course, this allows you to bet strong holdings just as aggressively as always, but you must make sure that your hand is more powerful than your sandbagging opponent thinks it is. You will find that when one of these players puts in the raise on the river, he has a huge hand,

and you can safely fold all but the most powerful holdings. You must be careful not to give the impression of being a player who will lay down hands that other players wouldn't even think of folding (like a set of Kings against what you positively believe to be a straight). The reason for this is that you don't want people making plays against you on the river. You can't afford to muck your hand in a large pot where you would have won (one time in 10 would usually be too often), so sometimes it is mandatory to demonstrate that you will call when you know you're beaten.

Hands that become wonderful against these players are draws to big hands. Straights and flushes that will make the best possible hands can often be played inexpensively because these players will attempt to slow-play big hands. Take all of the free cards that you need, and then punish them for their slow-play.

The other type of player I see sandbagging, is someone who slow-plays hands that just don't warrant it for a different reason. He may also have loose requirements for his starting hands. This gives you some disadvantages but more advantages. First, it is difficult to put him on a hand. If he is a loose caller as well, you can't know when he has improved to the point that his hand is better than yours. For instance, the flop comes 7♥4♦Q♣, and you have A-Q. When another 4 comes on the turn, he may show you 5-4 off-suit after he raises you on the river. You will be entering most pots with superior hands, though. It's important that a player like this has **some** difficulty putting you on a hand. He cannot know that you'll roll over big cards all of the time, and he must know that you will bet the absolute nuts into him. You should occasionally show down a winning hand with sub-standard cards. Make sure that your hand is suited, and that you are getting good value for your play. Remember, you are hoping to win any hand that you play, so if your sandbagging opponent limps in for $2, and you have the button with no callers in between you and your opponent, try throwing in a raise with a hand like K♥2♥ or 8♣5♣. You probably don't have the worst of it against this player, and he will be unable to put you on a hand later if you get to show it down. If you win the hand without a showdown, great, you could have had Aces. You don't have to run a bluff the whole way if you don't get a favorable flop. It may be prudent to give up on the play if you think you're beat. You should be able to steal the pot if big cards fall on the flop, but you really want to bury him with a straight or a flush. You will get plenty of action from the rest of the table for some time following this play, so be careful with the number of semi-bluffs and bluffs you try because you **will** be called.

Basically you want to control this player through strength. Bet your sets, straights, and flushes into him along with your other strong holdings. You can frequently bet four flushes and open-ended straights into him because you will often gain an extra bet on the river when *he* raises with a hand inferior to your made straight or flush. With medium holdings, bet them as well, but if he raises, and he hasn't started getting tricky, you should usually fold. Watch the player for tells regarding the strength of his hand. When you've got him, make him pay as dearly as possible. Sure, he's going to draw out occasionally on your top pair holdings with one card to a straight. When he makes his weak straight and you have a full house you'll hit payday.

Playing Versus Players Who Don't Understand How To Protect Their Hands

When a player is new in his casino playing life, he will often not understand the concept of protecting his vulnerable hands. This refers to betting and raising with hands such as top pair with a good kicker, two-pair, or even 'sets' when flush-draws and straight-draws are likely to be involved in the pot. Some players would prefer to wait and see if their opponents' draws materialize before they feel comfortable with their hands. This is an extremely costly practice. A player like this never gets value for his good hands, as he fails to charge the drawing hands a price to hit their draws.

The other weakness a player like this may possess is that he will often take draws that are hopeless to worthless. So how are you to take advantage of this situation? You must recognize the difference between one of these players and a pure calling station. You may come across a player that is somewhat more developed in his understanding of the game, and he has stopped taking draws that are without merit. Keep in mind that, usually, a 'calling station' evolves into a player who doesn't know how to protect his hand. A later transition occurs when a fellow player tells him how he should play hands that need protection. For instance, he holds A♦K♥, and the flop comes K♠8♣7♣, and someone bets into him. He just calls and a Jack comes on the turn and then he loses to someone holding J♦8♦. Someone at the table will say after the hand, "You should have raised to get out the J♦8♦. He wouldn't have called!" The next time this same situation arises, the player will go out onto a limb and raise. With the positive reinforcement of probably winning even more money than usual, or merely controlling the action of another player, this person will quickly adapt the technique of protecting his hands.

I believe that the key to optimizing your betting strategy is to study the player closely. If he doesn't have any physical tells when the flop comes or when he bets, you will have difficulty knowing when he has a strong hand. If you keep a close eye on him whenever he shows down a hand, you should be able to tell how far along in his evolutionary cycle he has come. If you find him taking draws to the low end of gut-shot straights when there is only $6 in the pot, he is probably closer to a calling station, and you can play as recommended in that section. If he is only taking the better draws with more respectable starting hands, but still doesn't quite understand raising with a hand like Q♦10♠ when the flop comes 10 high, then you need to adopt a different strategy.

Much of your strategy depends on your position vís a vís this opponent. These players are more likely to bet with a hand than raise with the same hand. This gives you a dilemma when you must act first because you really won't have a solid read on the quality of his kicker — assuming you can put him on top pair — if you lead bet and he calls. Contrast this with the instance when he doesn't necessarily have anything. If you don't bet you might give a free card which could beat you. It seems apparent that you would prefer to have this player be to your right, so that you can use him as a springboard to raise his bet when you have a hand like top pair. If an aggressive player is seated to either side of your opponent, there is a better chance to get protection when you bet. If there is another passive player to either side of your opponent, go ahead and bet your hands, but prepare to be run down on occasion. The times you are paid off when your hands hold up will more than pay for the times you get out-drawn by unlikely cards. Also, keep in mind that if one of these players raises, he probably has a very strong holding and isn't concerned about being beat, so you can safely fold all but your strongest hands.

Playing Versus Studied And Skillful Players

Regardless of what you may read in other literature, there are skillful players in the $2-$5 games. Some authors take the stance that if you are in a low-limit game you will be facing nothing but weak players. While the level of competition is not as tough at a typical low-limit table, this doesn't mean that you won't encounter quite adroit competition on a daily basis. Remember that the $2-$5 game is the only game in town, and not everyone wants to relocate just to play high limit poker.

As with most players, the skillful ones who extensively study go through transitions as they try to hone in on the optimum strategies for the game. Most of the literature available on hold'em is written, not only for tougher games — where *most* players have developed some skills — but for games where the betting is fixed. Both of these distinctions have the effect that while the expert strategy recommended in these texts is a winning strategy, it is not necessarily the optimum strategy. There are instances when the plays that work well in a fixed-limit game will cost you money and significantly raise your standard deviation in the $2-$5 game.

I will divide the studied and skillful players into two categories:

- The players who have yet to make the required adjustments to the spread-limit games.
- The players who have made those adjustments and are the experts of the game.

First, the players who have gone out and studied the excellent literature available on hold'em present interesting challenges to you as a player who has made more refining adjustments. What typically happens is that these players fail to take into account the reasoning behind the recommendations in these books, and they ignore the exceptions emphasized within the literature. Most of these breakdowns in correct applications center around semi-bluffing too frequently, and raising in situations where the raise doesn't accomplish the desired goal.

Many typical $2-$5 players enter the pot with strong starting hands without a raise, choosing to attack the pot after the flop comes. A player who enters the pot with a raise on the button with something like 7♥8♥ may find themselves facing a heads-up confrontation with someone who holds A♠K♠ or even a pair of Queens. This is a lousy situation. Also, someone who raises in early position with something like A♦J♠ or A♦Q♠ might get the correct results at first. When the other players discover that this player raises with these hands, he will be bombarded with callers. Large groups of players will be happy to play 5♦6♠ against a rotten old A♦Q♠ for $7! Now this is exactly where A♦Q♠ doesn't do well, in a large, multi-way pot. Strangely, it works out better to raise up front (very rarely) with cards like 7♥8♥ because it is more liable to put you in a desirable position.

While these are arguments to be wary of making these plays, how do you adjust your play to capitalize on these errors? Primarily, you would be more inclined to enter the pot in early position without a raise with some stronger holdings **when this studied player is in late position.** You can then re-raise and try to isolate the hand to the two of you. It's important to keep in mind that just because a player hasn't adjusted to the structure of the $2-$5 game, he still can be a dangerous opponent once the play of the hand begins. He may correctly semi-bluff, or raise with a second best hand in an attempt to out-play you. This usually results in your giving him more action than you would give your weaker playing opponents. In fact, if these are the only holes you can see in his game, you will be better off confronting him from a position of hand strength while still playing your best game. Most of your money comes from the weak players, and you needn't risk too much money trying to out-play him. You do want to earn his respect, though, so he doesn't indiscriminately make plays at you. Once he has decided that you play well, your encounters will be fairly infrequent. He will give you credit for strong skills and strong hands.

If the player is not too far along in his studies, he will take on the qualities of an aggressive, but not maniacal player, and you can play accordingly. Again, a player of this type can play havoc with your standard deviation, and you should base your playing style on how well you can determine just exactly where your opponent is in a hand. If you frequently can't put him on a hand, or a play, you are often better off taking a conservative stance.

What about the player who truly has a handle on the game as it's spread and yet maintains poker skills that transcend the $2-$5 game? These are players who could (and do) play in the larger limit games throughout the country, but ordinarily they play locally. First, make sure that you don't mistake these players for the conservative, tight players that regularly beat the game for small amounts of money. Those aren't the players to whom I'm referring. These skilled players may actually play more hands than should seem prudent, and will have a good mix of aggressive and technically solid play, as they always consider their opponents. They can be tough to pick out immediately because you may not get to see their cards very often after the hand. Pay careful attention to the closely contested hands they do show down. If you see them making calls, and raises that are precarious, but usually ending up with the best hand, be careful. When these players are in the pot, they usually have a legitimate claim to it, whether it is a good draw, or a good hand. Any manipulations you make, on the basis of hand strength alone, will probably not gain you much from these players. They will generally realize what you are trying to do, and will adjust their play accordingly. You can throw in some deceptive plays to keep them from trying to run over you, but again, they will usually recognize these for what they are. When in doubt, defer to the quality of their hands, and wait for your opportunity to be against the rest of the field. This isn't to suggest that you need to roll over and play dead. What I'm referring to, for example, is when you bet out after the flop holding Q♦10♦ with the board showing Q♠9♠4♥, and your opponent raises. Seriously consider folding. If he doesn't have you beat already, he has too many ways to beat you — added to any other callers' chances to beat you — to warrant you to continue without **large** pot odds. Basically, play a sound game. A player like this will recognize your skill quickly, and give you credit for legitimate holdings as well. You are like two finely tuned sports cars speeding down a traffic-filled highway. Your opportunities to strut your stuff are quite limited. You can enjoy some interesting heads-up play with an opponent like this if you want to work on your advanced skills, but be prepared to pay the price with larger fluctuations.

Again, for advanced skills to work on a studied and skillful player, you must demonstrate a high level of thinking *recognizable* by your opponent. If he doesn't notice **your** skill, he'll play you as he would an overly aggressive opponent, and your plays will fail.

Suggested Format For Records

You should keep comprehensive records on your play, both for tax purposes, and in order to keep an eye on your performance. The following is a suggestion for the information that will be important to you.

Field	*Example*	*How to Calculate*
Date	6/17/96	
Game	Hold'em	
Location	ABC Casino	
Limit	$2-$5	
Hours	3.5	
Win/Loss	$32	
Avg.	$10.45	=Tot (W)/Tot (H)
Session Avg.	$ 9.14	=Line6/Line5
Hours	3.5	
$(W_i)^2/H_i$	292.5714	= $(Line6)^2/H_i$
U 29.14		
Sigma (σ)	80.325	Standard Deviation
%(Win/Loss)	68.5%	#Wins/n

n = number of sessions
i = session number
Tot = Total
W_i = Win (in dollars session (i))
H_i = Hours (session (i))

A Few Final Thoughts

The information provided in this book should allow you to play $2-$5 Texas hold'em as well as most skillful players in the game. You will want to study other texts on hold'em and you should. The more you understand poker theory the more valuable this book will be. Study the game. Play the game. Your level of poker knowledge will be taken up a notch or two.

When you sit down at a table, keep in mind that you cannot judge the quality of a player by the way he appears. It is a mistake to make a snap judgment about an opponent and then not make any adjustments to how that person is playing presently. Just because a player enters pots with highly questionable starting hands, does not necessarily mean that he is a poor *poker* player. There are quite a few players who don't care at all about the stakes in a $2-$5 game, as they just want to play as many hands as possible in an evening for enjoyment. Some of these players can be skillful once the flop comes. They are usually aware that they are taking somewhat the worst of it, but they don't care.

The other suggestion I'd like to give you is to refrain from abusing other players at the table. People play for a wide variety of reasons, and most players are trying to play the best they know how while having what they consider to be a good time. The game *consists* of a unique two card concealed hand and a shared board of five cards. The fact that a player was an underdog after just seeing two cards, does not make him an idiot when he somehow turns a full house with these same two cards. A skillful poker player thrives in the environment of players who don't know what they're doing. Everyone should have a good time, and the expert will leave with most of the money (usually). Regardless of the cards that are out on the board, and the improbability of a given hand, you still must give a player credit for **something** if he is betting and raising even if it's just credit for being very optimistic.

<u>Glossary Of Terms</u>

Action	Bets and or Raises.
All-In	When a player no longer has chips available to bet.
Backdoor	Having a draw that requires that two running cards come on the turn and river.
Bankroll	Amount of money specifically for poker.
Blank	A card that doesn't help any hands.
Blind	Forced bet prior to seeing any cards usually to the left of the button.
Bluff	A bet or raise that can only win if no one else calls.
Button	The marker that designates the dealer.
Calling Station	A player who calls practically all bets.
Capped	When all bets and raises have been taken in a betting round.
Check	To pass, or not to bet.
Cheese	Lousy starting hand.
Cheques	Poker chips.
Drawing Dead	Having no opportunities to beat another player even if the hand improves.
Expectation	The probabilistic value (positive or negative) of any specific play or general strategy.
Fixed-limit	A game where the betting can only be one amount, before the flop and after the flop usually doubling after the turn, but remaining a specified amount.
Flop	The first three cards that are placed in the middle of the table that all players share.
Gut-Shot	Inside straight.
Handicapping	Assigning a numerical value to an event based on probability or odds. (i.e. 25%, or 3-to-1)
Heads-Up	When you are in the pot with just one other player.
Heater	Rush or series of winning hands. Also, 'sizz'.

Implied Odds	The amount of money that you can expect to gain from future betting actions. This value can be negative.
Lead Bet	Bet first.
Loose	Liberal playing standards.
Major (over-cards)	Aces and Kings.
Minor (over-cards)	Queens and Jacks.
Muck	Fold.
Open-ended	A straight-draw with a card on either side that will complete the straight.
Outs	Individual cards that will strengthen your hand to one that will beat your opponent.
Over-call	Calling when at least one other player has already called a final bet.
Over-Cards	Cards larger than those on the board.
Passive	Either a game that doesn't involve much raising or a player who doesn't often raise.
Pot Odds	The ratio of the amount of money in the pot to the amount of money you must put in to call a bet or raise.
Protecting Hands	Betting, raising or check-raising to eliminate players.
Raise	Putting at least double the amount of a previous bet in the pot.
Rake	The amount of money that the casino takes out of each pot.
River	The fifth and final card put on the board or widow.
Running	Two specific cards that come on the turn and river.
Sandbagging	Lying in wait with a powerful hand with the intention to raise any bet.
Semi-Bluff	A bet with more cards to come with a hand that probably isn't the best with the chances of turning into the best hand if the right cards come.
Set	Three of a kind when you hold a wired pair.

Show Down   1) A game where no betting or skill is involved.
                  2) Turning over your cards at the end of the
                  hand after all action has ended.
Slow-play   Waiting to bet, raise or take any aggressive
                  action until you have collected more money
                  from the players involved in the hand.
Smooth Calling   Calling as opposed to raising to entice other
                  calls or to avoid being re-raised.
Spread-limit   A game where any bet can be within a given
                  range of values.
Standard Deviation A measure of the dispersion or variation in a
                  distribution.
Sucked Out   Drawing-out or making a hand usually a draw
                  that has negative expectation.
Tip   The amount of money you give the dealer.
Toke   Tip.
Trips   Three of a kind when you have only one of the
                  cards in your hand.
Trouble Hands   K-J, Q-J, A-J, Q-10, K-10, and A-10.
Turn   The fourth card placed on the board or widow.

Under-The-Gun   The first player to the left of the big blind on the
                  first round of betting and first to act on any
                  round.
Weak-Tight   A player who is too quick to fold hands when
                  bet into or raised.
Wired Pair   A pair that a player holds with his two cards.

Outs And The Corresponding Odds

Remember: An 'out' is a card that will improve your hand to a winner.

Odds are expressed as *n*:1, that is, when I say a flush draw is 1.86, it means 1.86:1 against.

Outs on flop	% Chance	2 cards to come	Next card (after flop)	Next card (after turn)	Description
1	4%	22.50	46.00	45.00	
2	8%	10.88	22.50	22.00	Wired pair to improve to a 'set'.
3	12%	7.01	14.67	14.33	One over-card
4	16%	5.07	10.75	10.50	Gut-shot
5	20%	3.91	8.40	8.20	Pair & over-card
6	24%	3.14	6.83	6.67	Straight-draw versus flush-draw
7	28%	2.59	5.71	5.57	'Set' versus made straight or flush *on flop only*
8	31%	2.18	4.88	4.75	Open-ended straight-draw
9	35%	1.86	4.22	4.11	Flush-draw
10	38%	1.60	3.70	3.60	'Set' on turn to improve to full-house
11	42%	1.40	3.27	3.18	
12	45%	1.22	2.92	2.83	Flush-draw with gut-shot straight
13	48%	1.08	2.62	2.54	
14	51%	0.95	2.36	2.29	
15	54%	0.85	2.13	2.07	Open-ended straight-draw and flush-draw